The Essence of
FAMILY

THE MODERN BELIEFS SERIES

Kirsten Birkett

The Essence of Family
© Matthias Media, 2004

Matthias Media
(St Matthias Press Ltd. ACN 067 558 365)
PO Box 225
Kingsford NSW 2032 Australia
Telephone: (02) 9663 1478; Facsimile: (02) 9663 3265
International: +61-2-9663 1478; Facsimile +61-2-9663 3265
Email: info@matthiasmedia.com.au
Internet: www.matthiasmedia.com.au

Distributed in South Africa by:
Christian Book Discounters
Telephone: (021) 685 3663
Email: peter@christianbooks.co.za

Distributed in the United Kingdom by:
The Good Book Company
Telephone: 0845-225-0880
Facsimile: 0845-225-0990
Email: admin@thegoodbook.co.uk
Internet: www.thegoodbook.co.uk

ISBN 1 876326 89 1

Cover design and typesetting by Lankshear Design Pty Ltd.
Printed in Hong Kong.

Contents

Contents

Preface

THE MODERN BELIEFS SERIES

The world is shaped by what we believe: our values, our society, our daily activities will reflect what we believe to be true and important. This is the case for everyone, not just those who consider themselves 'religious' or 'having faith'. Whatever beliefs a person may hold, be they secular, atheist, religious, modern, traditional, scientific, artistic or a mixture of them all, that person's world view and way of life will reflect their underlying ideological conviction.

Most people go through life happily (or unhappily) unaware of their beliefs. It's easy to assume that what we think is what everyone does, or just never think about it at all. It's a sad way to be, both for individuals and for the society we create. If Socrates considered "the unexamined life is not worth living", we might add "the unexamined society is not worth having"— if we don't understand what we believe and why society is the way it is, we will never be able to affect it for the better.

The 'Modern Beliefs' series is not meant to be the final word on everything. It is meant to describe the essence of the beliefs that pervade our world; the ideas that tell us who we are, why we are here and what we ought to do about it. There are many such ideas, most of them inherited from past ages, some newly invented. We have no particular criteria for what comes under the heading 'Modern Beliefs'; if it has affected our culture today, it's worth understanding.

Our world is full of so many ideas it can be confusing just waking up in the morning. We hope that the 'Modern Beliefs' series will help to make at least a few parts of it more understandable.

About *The Essence of Family*

Most books on 'family' begin by trying to define it. Indeed, that's what many books and papers are entirely about. With a curious regularity, reference is made to Humpty Dumpty's conversation with Alice in *Through the Looking Glass*:

> "When I use a word", Humpty Dumpty said, in rather a scornful tone, "it means just what I choose it to mean—neither more nor less".
>
> "The question is", said Alice, "whether you *can* make words mean so many different things".[1]

The fact that this is quoted so often is interesting in itself. It seems to indicate that what most of these scholars are searching for is an understanding of what people mean when they use the word 'family'. That is, the search is not for a thing out there in the world, the thing that is unalterably 'family'; it is for something more elusive and potentially changeable. It is a search for what people, in whatever culture, sub-group or period of history they find themselves, regard as 'family'. Often, and more revealingly, it is a search for what the scholar thinks *ought* to be defined as 'family'.

Of course, words do mean what we make them mean—at least to some extent. One can legitimately use the word 'family' to refer to things as diverse as gangsters (a Mafia family) and letters on a page (a font family). But it is not totally arbitrary. Language is not infinitely elastic—you can't use 'family'

---

1. *The Complete Works of Lewis Carroll*, Penguin Books, London, 1988, p. 196.

to talk about paint stripper or ear wax. More importantly, the ways in which people live are not arbitrary or infinitely elastic. The basic unit of society in almost every culture known to man is a group of people related by blood or marriage, living together, with some degree of affection and loyalty.

I want to argue in this book that the parallels between cultures throughout history are no accident, and that there *is* such a thing as 'family'. Ultimately, I'll be suggesting that what gives unity and reality to human concepts of family is a God who has a family he loves.

This book is written from a Christian viewpoint, which may delight some readers and leave others less than enthusiastic. Why bring superstition, bigotry and blinkered ideology into the discussion, some may ask? Well, why indeed? I will be proposing that the Christian view actually has something very worthwhile—in fact, crucial—to contribute to the current debate about family. In my experience, the rejection of that view is most often not on the basis of rational debate or reflection, but is a result of thoughtless prejudice or rigid ideology. I ask of my readers only what any author longs for: that they apply their critical faculties to what follows, and attempt to leave their prejudice (even their anti-Christian prejudice) at the door.

My first task will be to outline—in brief—what the Bible's view of 'family' actually is, given that it is widely misunderstood and distorted in many discussions of the topic. (If, when you think of the 'biblical family' you think of white picket fences, you're wrong!) I will then look at the available data on families past and present, and compare the biblical perspective with others that are prominent in the current debate about 'family'. Following this, I will also look at how traditional Western ideas of 'family' are being challenged by emerging biotechnology, debates over sexuality, and feminism.

It will become obvious, I hope, that the biblical idea of family has a great deal to recommend it; that of all the alternatives proposed, it is the most workable and practical, and the most likely to lead to good lives for men, women and children. As well as this, I will argue that what the Bible says about families, and human beings in general, explains precisely why, in our post-Christian Western society, we are facing the problems we are.

To anyone steeped in twenty-first century Western secular values, it may well be that what the Bible says is very foreign. Our culture has strayed far from its biblical heritage, and most of us have been educated to reject the Bible as an authority. However, on another level, I suspect that what the Bible says may well resonate deeply with many of us, like a traveller in a foreign country who hears someone speaking his own language, and recognizes it as a voice from home.

Kirsten Birkett
SYDNEY, 2004

= *Part I* =

Defining
family

— 1 —
FAMILY IN THE BIBLE

Why should we start with a description of what the Bible says about family? Doesn't everybody already know? Isn't it a picture of 1950s America, with white picket fences, dad working full-time and never helping with the kids, mum at home baking cakes in a spotless kitchen and keeping a lipstick by the door so she can smarten up when she sees her husband walking up the front path?

Well, maybe not everyone puts the stereotype so bluntly, but it is nonetheless what many people assume to be the Bible's teaching on family. The Bible has been pilloried as patriarchal, oppressive, uninformed, outdated and, well, boring. That this picture can survive in the public mind is simply testament to the fact that very few public commentators these days actually know what the Bible says. We spend a whole chapter on it, therefore, so that we can clear the ground and know what we're talking about when we discuss the 'Christian view of family'.

Teaching about 'family' in the Bible occurs in many forms. We have examples of actual families, some good, some bad. We also have direct teaching, in the Old Testament and the New, about the responsibilities and duties of particular family members. The Old Testament Law is precisely that—a code of law that informs people not just how they should act but what to do when (as is expected) people behave badly. The New Testament also speaks directly to family members—

fathers, mothers, children—about attitudes and behaviour.

But this teaching about what families should be and do isn't presented as an isolated list of laws or rules, or even as general moral principles that should guide our lives. The Bible is an unfolding story, with a beginning, middle and end. It's the story of God and his unfolding purposes for the world, his action in the world, his speech to the world, his love for the world. To understand the Bible's teaching on family, we need to do more than simply work through the text chronologically examining every verse that contains references to family.

To have a *biblical* understanding of family means starting from the fundamental concepts, some of which the Bible does not reveal until the New Testament, when the hints and promises made by God early in the story (in the Old Testament) are brought to fruition at the story's climax (with the arrival on the scene of Jesus).

As we do so, we'll discover that family is much more than simply a manner of social organization. It is part of the fabric of the universe, a concept that involves relationships which will last into eternity and fulfil God's plans since the beginning of time. For in the New Testament we find out something utterly astonishing about God—that he is, himself, a family, a Father with a Son. *God* is the essence of family.

Let us begin, then, by sketching out the whole story, in broad brush terms, so that we can understand how 'family' fits into it.

The story of the Bible

We meet God in the very first line of the Bible. He created everything. This is a fundamental fact about God—he made the world, according to his own plan, creating and organizing everything in it. One of the things he organized was the special position of humankind in his creation. Humans are created beings, just like any other animal. But the human animal has a unique relationship with God, being in God's 'image' (Gen 1:27). As male and female, humans were given the particular honour and responsibility to rule the world as they multiplied and filled it (Gen 1:28).

God was pleased with the world he had created: "God saw everything that he had made, and behold, it was very good" (Gen 1:31). It suited his purposes exactly. The world, with all its beauty and pleasures, is a good place. However, although the Bible is clear on this point, and returns to it frequently throughout its pages, the main concern of the Bible is to explain what went wrong, and what God is doing about it.

It doesn't take much serious observation of the world as we know it to see that something *has* gone very wrong. For all the good in the world, we see just as much ugliness, evil and pain. Yes, there is beauty, but it is subject to decay. People accomplish great things, but they also get sick and die; moreover, we do horrendous things to each other and to other living creatures in the world. This is not a world that we would describe as unequivocally 'very good', as God did in Genesis 1:31.

We find out what went wrong in Genesis chapters 2 and 3. We are not given all of the precise details, but the gist of the matter is entirely clear. Humanity decided to claim for itself the world it had been given to rule under God. Male and female both decided to reject God and the wise instructions he had given them. How did they do this? Although it was the only thing in the world forbidden to them, humans ate fruit from 'the tree of the knowledge of good and evil'. They were not content with all the generous bounty God had given to them. They did not want simply to enjoy the good world;

they wanted moral independence in that world—they wanted to be in charge of knowing good and evil. Humans snatched moral autonomy, and so rejected God's right to decide what good and evil is.

It was a foolish rejection on many fronts. Firstly, God made the world, so only he could truly know how it worked—that is, what is good and bad to do in the world. Secondly, humanity already had absolutely everything given to them; it was greedy and unnecessary to make such a child-ish demand for independence. And thirdly, it was very foolish to reject the God who had so generously provided everything. Apart from anything else, it made him righteously angry.

Genesis 3 describes the results of this anger. God threw the humans out of the lush garden into the wilderness—a place where food would not be there for the taking, but where it would take hard and frustrating work to survive. He took away the former harmony between humans and their fellow created beings, so that the natural world became a hostile place. Most pertinently for this book, God cursed the rela-tionship between man and wife—the very closest relationship for humans, which had brought utter joy to Adam in the gar-den. The *only* thing 'not good' about creation had been the idea of the man being alone; creation was not truly complete until the woman brought him perfect companionship and the beginnings of family. But now, having rebelled against God, humanity was never to experience that relationship perfectly again in this world.

What was the precise nature of the curse upon family rela-tionships? Essentially, it was to create a power struggle between man and woman. Both were to struggle for domi-nance in the relationship (Gen 3:16); and the man would win. Here we see the kernel of tragedy for the rest of human history. Instead of living in mutual love, the two would fight; instead of the man using his natural strength to serve his wife, he would use it to dominate her. The story has been played out in millions of marriages, echoing throughout time.

But it's not all bad.

God is a loving God—that is precisely why the foolishness and rejection of humanity angers him so much. He truly wants the best for us, and has gone to amazing lengths to save us from the consequences of our own stupidity.

God's plan, which unfolds throughout the rest of the Bible, was to redeem humans from the slavery of violence and death that they brought upon themselves. He did it by becoming the perfect human himself—Jesus Christ, the only perfectly good man, who was representative of the human race, and therefore could take upon himself all the consequences of sin that humanity deserved. That is what Jesus' death is about—not just that it was a tragic and brutal way for a good man to die, but that he was actually God, dying, and then conquering death when he rose from the grave. He was the first to bring into reality God's plan for a new creation, one which would not be marred by death and enmity as this one is. The resurrected Jesus is the first example of what is offered to all of us—to come back to relationship with God in obedience to him, and so be part of a new creation, in which sickness and death are done away with, and where relationships are no longer marred by evil, selfishness and the desire to dominate others.

One of the amazing things we find out about God in Jesus is that God is a family in himself. God is a Father. Jesus is his Son. And when we come back to God, he doesn't just receive us as friends, he adopts us into his family. We discover that these ideas of family and fatherhood are not ultimately about biological relationships, although that is how they are worked out in humans. These concepts are something far more profound, at the deepest levels of the universe. In the very heart of God, he is a father who loves his son, and underwent terrible suffering in order to widen his family to welcome in any number of adopted children. We are not only saved from the consequences of our sin when we follow Christ—we become members of the ultimate, cosmic family.

Everything we read in the Bible, then, is in the context of this overarching and wonderful plan. What we have in this world are the decayed remnants of our originally good creation. Many good things have survived, but nothing perfectly. We are given plenty of advice about how best to live in this world, but always with the understanding that no amount of effort will actually create the perfect world that we all crave. We are all given the opportunity, however, to accept the promise of a new world in which the problems of evil will be overcome. That is what most matters in this world.

In the meantime, while we wait for the day which God has appointed for the curse to be lifted—a date that nobody knows, but that we know is coming—the best way to live is according to the wisdom that the Bible gives us about how *this* creation works. This will not create heaven on earth. No amount of white picket fences will actually solve the fundamental problems of selfishness and anger that plague our hearts. The Bible is not about creating pleasant enclaves of family values. The overall problem of the world is far too desperate for that.

However, the liberating thing about ceasing our enmity with God, and being adopted into his family, is that we can now live in harmony with the one who created the world, and according to the structures and purposes he built into the world. We are freed to enjoy the world as it was created to be enjoyed. And even though that joy will still be mingled with suffering and heartache—because the world is still corrupt, and we ourselves remain flawed and imperfect—living God's way will still be best in his creation, and will yield the most joy and satisfaction. It will always be a much wiser choice to work *in tune* with the principles on which the world is based, than deliberately *against* them.

So, in this context of a world which is imperfect and which ultimately will be superseded, what is the best way to live? How were we made to live with each other? We begin by looking at how God's people structured their community under God's instructions in the Old Testament.

Families in ancient Israel

Israelites defined themselves as one family, because they had one father—they were the children of Abraham. Their national identity as the group which was God's chosen people depended on their connection to a father, who had been promised these descendants by God. Although the Bible testified to the fact that *all* humans were related (see, for instance, the Table of Nations in Genesis 10), the nation of Israel had a special relationship with God. And the identity of the people of Israel depended on one man, their father Abraham.

Within this nation were sub-groups, again determined by kin relationships. The tribes were descendants of the twelve sons of Jacob (or 'Israel' as God later re-named him). These tribes were the basis of the main geographical and political sub-groups of the nation Israel. Within each tribe, individuals were also identified by their belonging to a clan, and then to an individual family—the closest concept to our modern, Western idea of the 'nuclear family'.

We tend to define the nuclear family as 'mum, dad and the children'. In some ways the description is a matter of linguistic ease and convention, but it also reflects our modern individualistic and matriarchal philosophy. In our modern view, a family is a group of equally defining elements—male parent, female parent, and male or female children. If anything or anyone is at the centre of the family, it is mum. She is the one who essentially changes this group of people from being any old collection of individuals to being a family.

We have been conditioned, then, to react with shock to the patterns of the Bible, in which the centre of the family is a father. The smallest kin grouping within Israel was, literally, 'house of a father' (*bêt'ab*). The person who defined a group of co-habiting people as being a family-unit, rather than any other group, was the father.

In Israel, there was no family without a father. In fact, you could say that a family is almost *defined* in the Bible as a group of people with a common father. They would physically live in his tent (if nomads) or his house (if settled). In any one household, this father might also be grandfather or great-grandfather, as his sons and grandsons married and brought their own wives and families into the fold. There may also have been slaves, servants and adopted children, with or without their own families. All these were members of the household of the father.

Judges 17-18 provides a picture of one such household. Micah the Ephraimite was the head, the father. He lived with his mother, a number of sons, a wandering Levite whom he had engaged as a priest, a number of men for defence of the household, and probably wives and children of many of these men. He lived in one building; he also had a shrine and a residence for the priest, and houses for all the men. All these buildings were entered through the one gate, so presumably there was a wall around them all. This arrangement, of clusters of dwellings or houses, either freestanding or sharing walls, with entrance through a central courtyard, is typical of residences discovered through archaeology.[1]

The father was central to the concept and the existence of the family in the Bible. He was the head—the source of the family, and the one who held it together. When the father was acting in line with God's ways, his position was one of generosity and responsibility for the wellbeing of all his family. Some of the worst examples of patriarchal abuse are seen when fathers ignored these instructions, instead copying the power-hungry ways of the surrounding cultures, in particular the Amorites, whose cruelty had led God to order their destruction (Gen 15:16).

The Ten Commandments demonstrate in condensed form what is spelt out in considerable detail in the Old Testament law. We see first of all the importance for his descendants of what the father does; indulging in idolatry, for example, will bring punishment to the third and fourth generations (which is probably his entire living household). The father is not to exploit or burden his family, by making them work while he rests on the Sabbath. Also, he must not covet or seize a neighbour's property; he is not to be greedy for power or influence. These basic commandments are followed through in numerous examples, as particular cases are dealt with in the law.

1.   Daniel I. Block, 'Marriage and family in ancient Israel', in Ken M. Campbell (ed.), *Marriage and Family in the Biblical World*, Intervarsity Press, Downers Grove, 2003, p. 40.

A husband and father, whether he was the head of the entire household or a son of that household, had responsibilities towards the whole family. He was charged to keep Yahweh's law and remember Yahweh's deeds, teaching his family by word and example. He was to provide for and protect the family, and work towards justice and harmony both within and outside the family group.[2] He had authority, and was deserving of honour, but the rule of the father was not his only or even primary characteristic. He ruled insofar as he was also uniquely responsible for the well-being of his family, and called upon to do all in his power to facilitate their life and flourishing. He was at the centre of the family, rather than ruling over it from a lofty height. It has been suggested that *patricentric* is a more accurate description of this reality than the more usual *patriarchal*, with its connotations of oppressive, lordly rule.[3]

Marriage

Of course to become a father, a man needs a wife. Weddings in the Bible are times of rejoicing—not at all unusual in any human culture, but worth reminding ourselves of, in our culture which is at best ambivalent towards marriage. The husband promised fidelity to his wife, and to provide for her sustenance, as part of a covenant of God between husband and wife (Mal 2:14). Song of Songs probably shows examples of the kinds of songs that would accompany a wedding, as the bride and groom were accompanied to the marriage chamber, where he would give her the gift of his seed, just as she would (hopefully) in time give him the gift of a child (e.g. 1 Sam 2:20; Ps 127:3).

2. See Block, *ibid.*, p. 47.
3. This is Block's suggestion; *ibid.*, p. 43.

This ideal of marriage springs, as we have seen, from the 'original' marriage of man and wife in Genesis 2: "Therefore a man shall leave his father and his mother and hold fast to his wife, and they shall become one flesh" (v. 24). There the pattern is set up that a man will leave his mother and father; those relationships are no longer primary to him, although they still exist. Instead, he "holds fast" to his wife—he not only joins with her, but there is a sense of duration and ongoing relationship. Genesis 2:25 also tells us that Adam and Eve were naked and felt no shame. This kind of willing vulnerability without fear of exploitation describes a perfect giving of oneself to each other. It is a necessary part of becoming "one flesh"—no longer being essentially two separate individuals, but in some sense becoming one unity. This *oneness* seems to be the chief purpose of marriage, and it is accomplished, to a significant extent, by having sex. The fact that a sexual relationship creates unity is also behind the law in Deuteronomy 22:28-29, which asserts that if a man rapes a virgin then he must marry her. (The principle is later reinforced by the apostle Paul in 1 Corinthians 6, as part of his prohibition of prostitution.)

Although the biblical pattern of marriage was originally monogamous (Gen 2), it seems that the Israelites often followed surrounding cultures in breaking this ideal. Nonetheless, the law insisted on certain curbs to this behaviour, and set standards to protect the dignity of the women involved (e.g. Exod 21:7-11). As God's self-revelation unfolds, it becomes clear that polygamy did not measure up to God's standard. The seventh and tenth commandments, given on Mount Sinai, reinforce the exclusive sexual nature of marriage; and Leviticus 17-26 suggests that part of being a complete person is sexual faithfulness. Adultery is one of the most serious crimes in Israelite law. It is seen as not only a break of trust, but as something that defiles humans and the community. It destroys the one body which is husband and wife, striking at the heart of the marriage commitment of openness and honesty. In Israelite law, the penalty for adultery is death (Deut 22:22).

In the book of Hosea, chapters 1-3, God's relationship with Israel is likened to a marriage. The same word, *b'rit* (covenant), is used to describe both relationships. There are many parallels between God's 'monogamous' love for Israel and marriage, especially in contrasting the exemplary patience and faithfulness of God with the promiscuity and apostasy of Israel.

Divorce was covered by law, although there are no actual examples of divorce described in the Old Testament. It was certainly not to be an easily accepted option; Malachi 2:16 expresses God's disapproval of the practice, as does Jesus in the gospels (Matt 19:8).

Unlike many other ancient civilizations, Israel saw no incompatibility between respect for fatherhood and the essential equality of men and women. Both men and women were created in the image of God, and both were charged with multiplying and bearing fruit, and having dominion over creation (see Gen 1:26-28). The woman was created of the same substance as man, in order to complete him, since the one thing in creation that was "not good" was the man's aloneness (Gen 2:18-23). He needed a companion, one of his own status and nature.

As we have seen, this relationship was hurt by sin, and the curses of Genesis 3 anticipate the particular way in which sin will work itself out in the marriage relationship. The woman will defy her husband, and in response he will exert mastery over her, instead of the godly, responsible leadership he is supposed to exercise. But the ideal remains, and is frequently recognized in biblical examples. The Song of Songs, for instance, shows a man and wife relating to each other as sexual equals, sharing the joy of love and sex. Proverbs 1:8 and 6:20 call upon children to listen to the teaching of their mothers, as well as fathers, and to benefit thereby. Fathers and mothers shared the job of bringing up children and defending them where necessary.

The Israelite community ascribed high honour to mothers as well as fathers. The famous passage at the end of Proverbs 31 is a telling testimony to this, but it is not a lone voice in the Old Testament. Clearly women could be seen as competent rulers and responsible members of the community. When Barak cowardly rejected his God-given role as leader, Deborah was gifted and competent to take his place, however improper she felt this to be (Judg 4-5).

Whole families were involved in the worship of Yahweh. In Nehemiah 8, we see men and women, and children old enough to understand, attending the reading and exposition of the Torah and the festival that followed. God's designs for worship did not separate men from women, unlike the temple that Herod later built, with its separate seating areas for the sexes.

Marriage was the way to produce godly offspring (Mal 2:14-15), children raised with knowledge of and obedience to God. Fathers and mothers named children, something much more important in Israelite culture than in modern Western culture. Israelite names generally meant something, and often expressed fidelity to God. Fathers were responsible for consecrating their first-born sons to God (e.g. Exod 13:2) and circumcising their sons on the eighth day (e.g. Gen 17:12). They were to raise children in knowledge of the Lord (e.g. Deut 6:6-9), and to teach them wisdom (Prov 1-9). They generally arranged marriages for their sons and daughters (although this was not mandated by law), and provided for them (a proper inheritance for sons, and a dowry for daughters).

Children

One way in which ancient Israel stands out as a beacon in the ancient world is that they did not kill their children. Unlike surrounding countries, Israel did not sacrifice children to their God, and regarded the practice as abhorrent. Nor did they expose unwanted children to die; in fact, the concept of 'unwanted' children is essentially foreign to the Bible. Children were richly desired blessings from God, something to be very thankful for.

The high value ancient Israelites placed on children was based on several deeply-held principles. First, every human being was in the image of God, and one of God's gifts to enable humans to carry out his charge to govern the world (Gen 1, Ps 8). Murder was forbidden precisely because humans are in the image of God (Gen 9:6), and this value on human life held for children, born or unborn, as well as adults. Also, God had instructed humanity to populate the earth (Gen 1:28; 9:1, 18-19). Moreover, although the basics of reproductive biology were certainly understood, children were thought of as a specific product of divine action. Childlessness was therefore a curse, and childbirth a gracious gift to be received with thanksgiving as evidence of divine favour.

The importance of children was also related to the Israelites' possession of the Promised Land. The physical land of Israel was God's holy place for his holy people, and children ensured the perpetuation of the family line in God's land, and the possession of the allotted inheritance. It was a terrible thing to have one's name disappear from Israel; this was the crime of Onan (Gen 38), who refused to impregnate his brother's widow, and therefore denied him the chance to have offspring.

A great deal of effort was devoted to the proper training and education of children. The book of Proverbs demonstrates the importance placed on teaching wisdom to the young. The goal was not to produce 'successful' children in the modern sense of high achievers, but to enable the child to become a wise person, secure in the right knowledge of God, and equipped to live skilfully and successfully in God's world. "The fear of the Lord is the beginning of knowledge", Proverbs 1:7 asserts at the beginning of the book. The alternative is to be a fool, and the fool is not only morally deficient but is likely to starve and come to disaster as well. Children were precious. They were not to be wasted, but brought up to fulfil their potential in proper service of God.

The Old Testament picture of family has a father at the centre, initiating and establishing his family. With his wife he runs the household of servants, slaves and extended kin; between them, husband and wife take care of domestic and community business, teaching their children and other dependants about God, and taking part in the worship that the whole community owed to God.

That was what was meant to be. Being sinful people, the Israelites frequently shirked their responsibilities and abused their power. Men abused wives and children; wives were disloyal to husbands and community; and children failed to obey or respect parents. When they failed to follow the proper pattern of family, Israel paid the penalty. Anguish, personal and community suffering, and even murder and death, were the consequences of family relationship breakdown (witness, for example, the archetypal sibling rivalry of Cain and Abel, or the tawdry drama of Genesis 38, in which Onan is only one of those to cover himself with shame).

The Bible not only holds out the biblical ideal; it is also

gritty in its realism about what happens when humanity ignores the God-given pattern of family relationship.

Family in the New Testament

The New Testament is considerably shorter than the Old Testament, and does not contain the long historical accounts, emotional outbursts of poetry and song, and prophetic histories so evident in the Old Testament. The New Testament proceeds on the assumption that the Old Testament is a true word from God, to be trusted and obeyed, but which by itself is incomplete. The New Testament is most concerned with describing how Jesus fulfilled the promises of the Old Testament and overcame the shortcomings of its covenants.

However, the New Testament also contains moral teaching which builds on the Old Testament and clarifies what is essential. It is not a different picture from the Old Testament, but it does, importantly, expand the idea of family so it can be seen in its eternal context.

Fathers and husbands

The New Testament affirms the Old in its emphasis on the responsibilities of fathers to teach and encourage their children, and to love their wives. Indeed, the apostle Paul puts this in the strongest of terms: a husband must be prepared to lay down his life for his wife, just as Jesus did for the church. The husband's headship must be on the same terms as Christ's headship: self-sacrificial care and nurture, even to the point of death, so that his wife might not only be physically cared for, but spiritually presented as worthy of heaven on the last day (Eph 5:21-33).

Fathers are to instruct and discipline their children, so they might properly know God. In doing this, they are not to frustrate their children, because doing so would not only be counter-productive, but irresponsible as a loving father (Eph 6:4; Col 3:21). In describing his ministry to the Thessalonians, Paul reveals what fathers should be like: "For you know how, like a father with his children, we exhorted each one of you and encouraged you and charged you to walk in a manner worthy of God" (1 Thess 2:11-12). The generosity and care characteristic of even flawed, human fathers is the point of Jesus' parable in Matthew 7: "Which one of you, if his son asks him for bread, will give him a stone? Or if he asks for a fish, will give him a serpent? If you then, who are evil, know how to give good gifts to your children, how much more will your Father who is in heaven give good things to those who ask him!" (Matt 7:9-11).

Marriage

Jesus also affirmed in no uncertain terms the Old Testament importance of marriage as a life-long, monogamous commitment (Matt 5:32; 19:1-12; Luke 16:18). This is followed through in the New Testament, in the teachings of the apostle Paul, for instance. Marriage in Paul's view is a matter of true interpersonal trust and equality. Nonetheless, Paul acknowledges the problems that are inevitable for marriages in a fallen world, and he wants his people to be free from these anxieties. Marriage is good and to be embraced, but it will also bring difficulties and worry, and will tend to compete with a whole-hearted devotion to God. In light of their current position, poised between the first coming of Christ and his imminent return, Christians do well to remain as they are, says Paul, including remaining single (see 1 Corinthians 7 for an extended discussion).

Nonetheless, Paul is a realist about the impracticality of

some—perhaps even most—Christians remaining single. If we can't control ourselves, better to marry "than to be aflame with passion", he says (1 Cor 7:9). And for those who do marry, Paul paints a wonderful picture of mutual care and respect. A married person's body belongs to his or her spouse. Each partner owns the other's body. What follows from this, however, is not the selfish claiming of the other person's body, but the opposite—because a husband knows that his body actually belongs to his wife, he must give himself unsparingly to her in sexual relationship, to satisfy her (and vice versa). Sex is absolutely crucial in Christian marriage; it is necessary, good and meant to be frequent.

In Ephesians chapter 5, Paul further expands the significance of marriage. He quotes Genesis 2 in order to affirm that there is a profound unity between husband and wife, such that the two are 'one flesh' or 'one body'. And he applies this idea to the union between Christ and his church. They too are 'one body', and Christ cares for his body by laying down his life for her. In the same way, husbands should care for and nourish their own 'bodies' (that is, their wives) in sacrificial love. In fact, Paul goes so far as to imply that the marriage between Christ and his people is the perfect loving marriage that Genesis 2 looked forward to, and that human marriage is a type or analogy of this divine relationship between Christ and his people.

Children

Children are not often explicitly addressed or described in the New Testament, but their innate value, and the importance of bringing them up well, is reinforced. Jesus famously accepted children as worthy of his time and attention: "Let the little children come to me and do not hinder them, for to such belongs the kingdom of heaven" (Matt 19:14). Children are even held up as in some ways understanding reality more clearly than adults, acknowledging their dependence upon others and being willing to trust their father, in the way that adults should trust their heavenly father, without suspicion or wilful independence (Matt 18:1-6).

The particular teaching about children reinforces the Old Testament view: that children are to obey their parents and listen to them, and parents are to teach them responsibly (Eph 6:1-3). A man's ability to care properly for his children is seen as a necessary qualification for running a church in 1 Timothy; if he is neglectful of his family, he should certainly not be allowed a position of responsibility in the church family.

The family in the new creation

The Bible is consistent in upholding the importance of family, and faithfulness within it. However it has more to say about family than just describing it as an ideal social structure. The Old Testament gives some of the theological meaning of family, but it is in the New Testament that we understand it best. Marriage is not just a socially helpful way to live—it reflects the ultimate reality of a relationship between the Son of God and the people he has saved. 'Family' is the concept by which we understand an eternal reality, the new creation to come in which Christ invites us to be adopted members of God's family. Ephesians 3:14-15 says: "For this reason I bow my knees before the Father from whom every family in heaven and on earth is named". There is a fundamental truth about every family on earth: God is the Father who names— that is, creates and determines the nature of—all families. This is not a vision of white picket fences. It is a profound insight into a cosmic reality that will last for eternity.

This world is not always going to remain as it is now. It is going somewhere. There is a plan, a purpose, an End to which the whole creation is heading. And we cannot understand anything properly (including family) unless we understand it from the point of view of the End, of where God is taking our world. Because Christ has come, proclaiming and inaugurating the kingdom of God, then nothing is quite the same any more.

For now, we live in this created world like any other creature, and we participate in it, and enjoy its goodness with thanksgiving. We enjoy marriage and family. The husband-wife bond is precious—but not just because that is how God created us to live. We discover in Ephesians 5 that it is a reflection of the infinitely precious relationship between Christ and the church. It is a loving, sacrificial and godly bond, which is the ideal situation for bringing up godly—and therefore most fully human—children. The family as a whole is also precious, being the metaphor that God the Father uses to describe his relationship with his redeemed people. He is not just King and Saviour—he welcomes his people as their Father, allowing them an undeserved entry into his very house, as his adopted children.

In a fallen world, family protects the weak and echoes God's boundless love. It is essential to being the creatures we are. Things will be different in the next world—there will be no marriage between man and woman, only the ultimate marriage between Christ and his church. For that reason, people might choose to live only for that marriage, and so be undistracted by human marriage bonds in this world. That is a valid and available option. But it is a decision that few will make, and it involves overriding our created nature, which is still made for this world. Here in this age, we are created in families, and generally function best in that context. Because of sin, families can be damaged and fractured, their wonderful love poisoned into crippling hate. This is what sin does, making the most potent weapon from the most precious gift. The hatred that can result from the breaking of families is testimony to the great love that families inherently have. We are born into families, and we are meant to live in them. Broken and painful as they may be, families remain the way we were made to live, and no human structure really replaces them.

But valuable and crucial as family is, there is a greater priority. This was emphasized by Jesus in Luke 14:26. "If anyone comes to me and does not hate his own father and mother and wife and children and brothers and sisters, yes, and even his own life, he cannot be my disciple." He made a similar point in Mark 3:34-35, when he gave the family of believers priority over his own blood family: "And looking about at those who sat around him, he said, 'Here are my mother and my brothers! Whoever does the will of God, he is my brother and sister and mother'".

In the Bible, the overarching goal of the world—to bring people into a new creation, under Christ—is what matters most. Everything else must come second, even such God-given gifts as families. This is not permission or mandate to neglect family, if you have one. Stephen Barton's description is perceptive on this point:

> How does this passage [Mark 3:34-35] speak to modernity? To say that it speaks 'against' the family is to go too far. Exegetically, such a view fails to account for the rhetorical, hyperbolic aspect of Jesus' sayings, both here and elsewhere … it also overlooks sayings which manifestly support family ties (e.g. Mark 7:9-13; 10:1-12). Psychologically and socio-

logically, it is counterintuitive and even, in some contexts, irresponsible. Theologically, it contradicts the goodness of God in creation and the redemption of creation through the incarnation.

What this account *does* say to us, however, is that the family is *not an end in itself* and that modernity's 'idolatry of the family' stands under judgement. It affirms that belonging to Jesus and the 'new' family of Jesus—theologically speaking, the church—is the prior, more profound (because eschatological) reality to which human beings are called and in terms of which human relationships, including familial relationships, are to be judged. It says to us that children are important, not just for their parents' fulfilment, but because they are loved by God who in Jesus took them in his arms and blessed them (Mark 9:36-7; 10:13-16) and who entrusts them to parents and the church for their nurture and growth into mature human beings.[4]

In heaven, we will all be God's family, and the pattern of this world in which marriage and children is the norm will be changed (Matt 22:30). Nonetheless, we still live in the real world now. We can't disregard the order of this creation, even if it has problems because its good structures have been distorted by sin. The ultimate family is Christ and the church, heaven, God's family. As with many things, our human lives now reflect some aspect of heaven, the real thing is there. But we are still here in this creation. It is a blessing to have these echoes here; temporary as they are, they are still important.

---

4. Stephen C. Barton, 'Living as families in the light of the New Testament', *Interpretation*, 52/2, 1998, p. 138.

So what do we say to a hurting world, particularly in the area of family? It is not that salvation comes through a conservative fifties-style suburban life. Salvation only comes through Christ, and he is part of a far greater reality. Nonetheless, if the Bible is right—if what it says about family is true—then we would expect a deliberate rejection of this way of living to be bad for us. We would expect a lifestyle in opposition to this teaching to go wrong somewhere along the way, because it is in opposition to reality—to the way we are made, to the way the universe works.

The disaster of post-sexual revolution Western society would be just what we might expect.

⊶ 2 ⊷
FAMILY THROUGHOUT HISTORY

As we have seen, the Bible has a great deal to say about what families should be, and how they work best. This is not merely a social programme. The biblical view of family flows from the nature of God himself—a father, who loves his children and wants to create the ultimate family with them in eternity. God is the creator of everything, and his nature is reflected in what he has made. We were made for relationships, and family relationships that begin with the lifelong marriage of a man and a woman are the sort we were made for.

All that is very well, you may say, but is it realistic, let alone true? Is the biblical picture of family a desirable or useful one? Is it a normal way humans are meant to relate to one another? If we were to take our cue from most history and anthropology written since the 1960s, we would answer 'no' to all these questions. Many scholars have argued that the biblical idea of family is simply a late, twentieth-century American invention imposed upon the Western world. Margaret Mead, for instance, claimed in a famous study that in Samoa sexual faithfulness and monogamous marriage were not the norm at all, and that the resulting sexual freedom led to a healthier society with less crime. It was later discovered that her data was flawed, but her teaching that other cultures outside the conservative West rejected the biblical pattern and were better off for it, started a wave of trenchant criticism of traditional families.[1]

---

1.   Phillip D. Jensen, 'Coming of age in controversy: Margaret Mead, Derek Freeman and intellectual leadership' in *Prodigal World*, Matthias Media, Sydney, 2003, pp. 41-58.

Various other interest groups have tried to present human relationships as varying radically in different cultures and over different times. The conclusions that are drawn vary according to the particular ideological bent of the author, but lately you can almost guarantee that whatever the proposed model, the biblical ideal of married male-female parents will be rejected as an artificial, and ultimately harmful, construct.

Do they have a point? Is the biblical pattern an oppressive and destructive imposition on human nature and relationships? What does the history of 'family' tell us about this?

We cannot possibly survey every human culture in the space available here, but we can at least look broadly at some cultures from the ancient world onwards that have been the precursors of, or typical of, 'the West'. What kind of family structures do we find?

Family in the ancient world

It is not surprising that we find that societies geographically close to Israel in the ancient world have similar family arrangements. In most civilizations of the ancient world, a patriarchal structure existed but without the softening influence of the Israelite emphasis on care and responsibility rather than power. There is very little evidence to support the contention, sometimes voiced, that matriarchal social structures existed in the ancient Near East. Male rule of society and home was the norm in Egypt and Mesopotamia.[2] Generally the head of the household, or *paterfamilias*, had complete charge of the house-

2. Victor H. Matthews, 'Marriage and family in the ancient Near East', in Ken M. Campbell (ed.), *Marriage and Family in the Biblical World*, Intervarsity Press, Downers Grove, 2003, p. 1.

hold's family. He was responsible for the family's reputation and for representing the household in court.

Like Israel, the household of the ancient Near East included the extended family. The head of the household might live with his wife or wives, children, also younger brothers or sisters and perhaps a widowed mother. Some women could live outside of this structure—prostitutes, some widows—but consequently also did not receive the protection offered by a resident father or brother.

With the rise of monarchies in ancient Mesopotamia, evidence for class distinctions also begins to appear. Royalty could only inter-marry, and the priesthood stood outside ordinary marriage patterns. For the commoners, however, marriage was the norm. It was expected that every adult would become a contributing member of a household and the community. Parents would generally arrange the betrothal of children, within the same social class and economic standing. This would involve a contractual agreement to marry, including the giving of the bride-price (from groom's family to bride's). As the bride could be as young as twelve, she would not necessarily go immediately to live in her husband's household (men could marry as late as thirty), but the transfer of the bride-price meant that the marriage was considered binding under law. The dowry—paid from the bride's family to the groom's—would be of the same value as the bride-price, and went with the bride to her new home. It remained her property, and would be passed on to her children.

Although there is evidence of polygamy in certain specific cases, most Mesopotamian marriages were evidently monogamous. Polygamy seems to be mainly for reasons associated with infertility or illness on the part of the first wife. A priestess, for instance, might not be allowed to have children even though she could marry. In this case, another woman would bear children who would become the legitimate children of the marriage. A man was also free to enter into a second marriage if his first wife contracted an illness which made sex impossible. She could, if she chose, take her dowry and return to her father's house; if she did not so choose, the husband was obliged to support her. Divorce was possible, but overall marriage was considered a binding contract. Adultery was forbidden, as a violation of the contract and angering the gods.

Children were considered essential to marriage, and parallels were drawn between honouring one's father and the ability to become a father. The disobedient son could well be punished by finding himself infertile when the time came for him to marry. Children were spiritually necessary, to uphold traditions and perform the rituals of the ancestor cult. They were also financially necessary, to work the fields. Infertility was considered a catastrophe, and could be grounds for divorce. However, having too many children, particularly daughters, could also be a financial disaster. It was not uncommon for infants to be abandoned; daughters could also be given to the goddess as cloistered priestesses. Abandoned children could be adopted by childless couples, or more sinisterly, raised as slaves for sale.

Many similar customs are found in ancient Greek and Roman society. Of course, Sparta was different, with its intensely militaristic culture in which men were segregated from age seven, and even after their marriage at age twenty would live in army barracks. However, even other Greeks regarded Sparta as an anomaly, even though many admired it as a particularly efficient state.

Greek and Roman writers saw marriage and the procreation of children—within marriage—as fundamental to human society. Cicero considered its rules to be shaped by ancient custom and not to be tampered with—indeed for centuries Roman families were scarcely affected by statute law, being so thoroughly grounded in custom. The Greeks had tended to be somewhat more ruthless with family law in the interests of the state. Nonetheless the basic family structures remained remarkably similar.

Athenians, from 451 BC, were only allowed to marry other Athenians. If not, their children could not be Athenian citizens. This very pragmatic approach to marriage, coloured by overwhelming loyalty to the city-state, is typical of the ancient Greek family customs. Athenian men would commonly keep mistresses, before and after marriage, and romantic love often seems to have flourished there. Marriage, on the other hand, was about legitimacy and continuation of the state. For this reason, sons were generally more important than daughters (Herodotus states at one point, "Cleomenes ... died childless, leaving behind only a daughter"[3]). Sons inherited equal portions of their father's estate, on the whole, but daughters who inherited were expected to marry a male member of the clan.

If a generalization might be made about ancient Greek families, their legal structure was often manipulated by the state for pragmatic reasons, and so marriage and family could seem loveless. Nonetheless, the fact that the pragmatic state policy continued to use family as its primary social structure indicates the stability and strength of the institution.

The Middle Ages
Families are evident from late antiquity, and what evidence there is shows that they could be loyal and loving and fair.

3. Quoted in S. M. Baugh, 'Marriage and family in ancient Greek society', in Campbell, *ibid.*, p. 130.

Women worked outside the home when male labour was short, especially as the population declined in the later Roman Empire due both to pagan practices of contraception, abortion and exposure of unwanted children, and Christian celibacy, virginity and chastity.

There was a resurgence of paternal authority in the High Middle Ages, and patrilineage (descent through the male line) and primogeniture (inheritance by the first-born son) were common. These domineering tendencies, based more on economic greed and the wish to keep property than on any real concern for family relationships, strained the family system somewhat. Even so, families persistently survived and insisted on leaving evidence of loving, companionable and sentimental marriages. Popular songs and poetry, elite literary chronicles, and letters and anecdotes, all give evidence of families enjoying close emotional lives.

The story of families from the middle ages into the early modern period is somewhat of a battleground in itself. For some time, the years 1400-1800 have been held up as the hatching grounds of the nuclear family finally realized in the twentieth century. During this time, certain social developments affected family life. Economic developments gradually led to a separation of home and workplace, as cottage industries and the agricultural society gave way to the industrialized, urban society. Servants as part of the household declined and eventually virtually disappeared. The family became more of an isolated unit, withdrawn from public life. Indeed, the home was a retreat from life; a haven of private comfort. What commentators have made of these changes has differed considerably. Many historians from the 1960s onwards considered this a beneficial movement—the modern, nuclear family was upheld as the ideal, as opposed to the pre-industrial, rigid, authoritarian, patriarchal family. Working desperately for survival, the pre-modern family was an impersonal place.[4]

The received view, then, for much of the twentieth century, was that families unambiguously changed for the better between 1400-1800. This was the period, it was claimed, in which steps from patriarchy to partnership began to be taken. Relationships could now be kinder and more equal.

But while this view was being developed, an alternative was being put forward by feminists. This perspective was somewhat negative to the pre-modern family, but *far more* negative to the modern family. In some ways, this view was just as biased by ideology as that which it replaced, but it did establish a balance in understanding pre-modern families. Pre-modern times were seen by feminists as in some ways more friendly to women, and perhaps even the best model of family achieved until the twentieth century. Feminist history generally regards the nuclear family as a patriarchal unit, and often values the older household-as-workplace model, with men and women working together and sharing childcare in the extended family and community family. Women were, indeed, able to work outside the home, and had a strong legal standing in many parts of Europe during the middle ages. After the plagues, the male workforce was depleted, and women learned and practised trades. In 1300, for instance, only three Parisian guilds explicitly excluded women. In other places guilds would explicitly exclude men.

Women's guilds could be very highly paid. Women's guilds of yarn makers, gold and silk embroiderers, and silk makers, were among the city of Cologne's most highly paid.[5] Women

---

4. Steven Ozment, *Ancestors: The Loving Family in Old Europe*, Harvard University Press, Cambridge MA, 2001.
5. *ibid.*, p. 24.

also did domestic chores, but there was no strict gender seg-regation of labour; in fact, married couples would often work together in home-based businesses. Women, single or mar-ried, could trade, market and officiate over goods; women in religious and quasi-religious vocations also had professional work. Married women often had citizenship, legal rights, property ownership and so on—that is, even more legal rights than non-propertied men (although their husbands on the whole had greater rights). But in criminal matters a woman had equal access to courts, and rape was recognized as a real crime. In matters of business, women spoke for themselves.

In all this, family structure remained traditional, based on marriage and the importance of children within marriage, and blessed by the church. Even so, there were also significant numbers of men and women, forgoing both marriage and children, in religious monastic life. Economic circumstances could fluctuate widely, affecting the fate of particular families. From the late fifteenth century, there was endemic poverty in Western Europe, which produced unemployment and vagrancy. The church was in a process of decay, and its once numerous hospitals and almshouses declined as a means of economic relief. Moreover, the craft guilds, which had for centuries acted in care of the poor, were in a process of disso-lution for economic reasons.[6]

However families remained, and continued to be places of close caring. Linhard and Katherine Tucher were separated from their seven children during a plague scare in Nürnburg in 1533. From the six month separation, while the children stayed with an aunt in another city, over two hundred letters

6.   W. K. Jordan, *Philanthropy in England 1480-1660: A Study of the Changing Pattern of English Social Aspirations*, Allen & Unwin, London, 1959, p. 56.

survive between the households. A letter from Augsburg merchant Leo Revensburg to his fourteen-year-old son in Paris, beginning an apprenticeship, included advice about keeping his feet dry and avoiding treacherous swimming holes, as well as career advice and warnings against immoral temptations.[7] Plague, war, social and economic upheaval caused all sorts of changes; but affectionate relationships amongst family households remained.

The sixteenth century was a time of social upheaval and religious dissent. There was more labour available, and small businesses found it harder to survive the competition from countryside and overseas trade. A significant aspect of the dissolution of the monasteries in England was that the tenants and servants of the monasteries were thrown upon a labour market already saturated. The new proprietors of monastic lands were far more efficient and so employed less labour. They were the ones who enclosed lands, grazed sheep and raised rents.

The agrarian revolution of the fifteenth century had changed the attitude of owners to land, increasingly seen as capital to be exploited. Landowners began to shift to a more economically rapacious practice, which lowered employment on the land. Sheep grazing also increased employment around the industrial centres, but those dispossessed of their traditional land lacked the mobility and skill to make the change. There was also a general increase in population from 1500, resulting in an overall surplus of labour.

This changed the family patterns of work, most notably for women. Women's apprenticeships declined, and home labour became more common. However, contrary to the feminist view, there is no evidence to suggest that women at the

7. Ozment, *op. cit.*, pp. 77-79.

time regarded this as a backwards step, merely a change in labour. Home labour would include the business of husbandry, slaughtering, preserving and cooking, tutoring, keeping records and so on—a far from dull employment, especially when compared to labour outside the home. The work pattern within families had changed, but this was not seen as any reason to change the basic structure of the family.

Some studies maintain that newly centralized governments and new religious systems put women in their place in the home, with serial pregnancies and no rights. The Lutheran family is seen as particularly authoritarian and totalitarian. This view, however, is not merely wrong, but quite ironic when it is considered that Luther himself strongly criticized oppression of women in ancient and medieval writers. His wife Katherine had several careers of her choice.

Marriage became more common during the fifteenth century, mainly due to increasing prosperity. There was some move away from strict parental control. The Protestant Reformation brought a new model of marriage which suited this move; marriage was seen as the expected godly lifestyle for adults, with only very few suited for celibacy. The Protestant Reformation and subsequent Puritan movements also led to the closing down of many brothels and public bathhouses, a move which did much to prevent the spread of syphilis. Protestants took the lead in rejecting ancient and medieval portrayals of women as inferior. Intellectual camaraderie and pragmatic equality in marriage were encouraged. Luther washed nappies and made beds, and made Katherine his heir.

Letters from Luther to his wife while he was away on theological business certainly do not read as letters to an inferior. Luther discussed theology and politics with his wife as one who would be interested in such things.

To Katherine Luther at Wittenberg

4 October 1529

Grace and peace in Christ. Dear Katie, know that our friendly conference at Marburg is now at an end and that we are in perfect union on all points except that our opponents insist that there is simply bread and wine in the Lord's Supper, and that Christ is only in it in a spiritual sense … Tell Bugenhagen that Zwingli's best argument was that a body could not exist without occupying space and therefore Christ's body was not in the bread, and that Oecolampadius' best argument was that the sacrament is only the sign of Christ's body … I have much to do and the messenger is in a hurry. Say good-night to all and pray for me. We are all sound and well and live like princes. Kiss little Lena and Hans for me.

Your humble servant

Martin Luther[8]

Luther also wrote to his children when away, telling them stories and sending his love.

Contrary to many modern views of history, it is difficult to see the fifteenth century onwards as a time of despair and loss for women. Things changed, and there were many general hardships in society, but society had not particularly changed for the worse as far as women were concerned. It was a time of deep public concern with the problem of poverty, with much discussion of its causes, extent and possible cures. The greatest problems came from urban poverty. Social moralists were mostly concerned with the rural poor; the Elizabethan

---

8.   Preserved Smith, *The Life and Letters of Martin Luther*, ed. Robert Backhouse, Hodder & Stoughton, Sevenoaks, 1993, p.192.

poor laws were framed principally to help them. But it was the urban poor who were the worst off, with real seasonal unemployment and cyclical periods of economic depression. English society was unprepared for this and could not understand it. Private charity did most to relieve this problem.

It has often been asserted that childrearing was oppressive and cruel in the medieval past, and only became humane in the twentieth century. In popular caricatures, Protestant parents were regarded as being particularly bad, teaching their children that they were sinful little wretches, and thus doing untold psychological damage. But as with the 'stifled' Protestant wives, evidence for downtrodden Protestant children is not prominent. Recognition of the special needs and stages of children has been documented back to antiquity; they were not uniformly treated as little adults. Household sources, letters and diaries testify to the existence of understanding parents in all kinds of societies and religions. There are bad examples too, of course, but there is no evidence of a universally bad treatment of children giving way to kindness and goodness in modern times. Certainly, from the early medieval period, there is documentation of happy family life and kind treatment of children, including the recognition of good and bad psychological effects on children. There are also records of parents mourning all dead children—it is a myth that medieval families were indifferent to children because of the high death rate. Parents would name and mourn stillborn babies, and keep them in family genealogies. Later medieval family archives record that the greatest fears of newlyweds were things such as sterility and miscarriage, and their greatest joys in parenting.

Certainly numerous reports of accidental death of children exist. There is at times a reasonable suspicion of criminal negligence or even murder by parents wanting to limit the size of families, or single women wanting to avoid the stigma of illegitimate children. Female children are underrepresented in several censuses (although this could be because daughters simply were not counted in the census). Nonetheless, few accusations or convictions for infanticide are recorded, and foundling hospitals thrived, suggesting that it was more likely that unwanted children would be given away rather than killed. It is likely that infanticide did occur, but it was by no means common or acceptable. (Actually, the figures for the modern world are far worse.)

There are many examples, during the Middle Ages, of tightly-knit families. Parents sent letters to children giving advice. There are stories of parental care and guidance, sometimes frustrated by youthful rebellion and set right by parental action.

Hamburg poet and literary editor Matthias Claudius wrote voluminously to his ten children. When his eldest child left home at sixteen, Matthias gave him careful advice.

> Be happy to learn from others, and where there is talk of wisdom, human happiness, light, freedom, and virtue, listen intently. But do not take what you hear for truth on the spot, for not all clouds carry water, and there are sundry kinds ... Accept nothing from pushers; where haranguing occurs on the street, move along.[9]

Medieval and early modern parents cared about their children. They based their theories of childrearing on an ideal of sound moral and spiritual foundation early in life. Quaker Mary Sewell expressed in a letter her delight in and love of children as she gave advice on religious instruction:

> The first thing to teach a little child is that he has a Father in heaven who loves him and wishes him to be as happy as

9. Ozment, *op. cit.*, p. 86.

he can be ... Do not too early impress upon the mind of a little child that he is a sinner.[10]

Moreover, what records there are (and there are quite a few from antiquity onwards) offer many examples of the 'modern sentimental family', which is often supposed to be a post-industrial invention. Records are more abundant from the fourteenth century onwards. Family archives, letters and diaries became much more popular and common. And when you study personal records, you find that spousal and parental love is by no means an invention of recent times. As we survey the medieval period, and indeed the periods preceding it, we find that the family as traditionally conceived, far from being a modern Western invention, has a long and established history.

The industrial revolution and onwards

The nineteenth century saw a great increase in theorizing about families. Socialist theorists made imaginative efforts to rethink the workings of love, motherhood and the social role of women. Evolutionary theories pondered the origins of society and the family.

A great deal has been made in feminist history of the nine-teenth-century doctrine of 'separate spheres'. This doctrine—that men were meant for the public sphere and women and children for the private, home-making sphere—is seen to be part of the rise of industrialism, where 'real' work was moved outside the home. As we shall see, the picture is far from clear-cut.

The nineteenth century is famous as the period in which

10. *ibid.*

great changes took place in women's lives, and the women's movement was born. At the same time, it is important to remember that peasant women accounted for nearly three quarters of the Western female population, and their lives probably changed little over the course of the century. Social changes were definitely taking place, with the advent of industrialism, but the family neither died nor was 'born'. Though much discussed, and subject to strain, it continued.

The preceding century, the eighteenth, had seen not only economic changes, but the radical political changes of the French and American revolutions. And even in those countries where the political revolution could not be dated so precisely, there was still a shift towards modernity and democracy, and away from monarchy.[11] Wives took a place in the French and American revolutions, alongside their husbands. French women were firebrands of revolution; they led marches and rallies, and incited the men to join them. American women boycotted English goods, and would spin yarn for the country.

The American revolution saw a call for women to have a place in the country's life, to be independent, self-reliant, and educated—this is evident in various works of literature. Why? Precisely so that they could be strong mothers, playing a civic role in raising sons to be good citizens. The republican mother was the feminine ideal in French society as well.[12] European travellers to America in the nineteenth century

11. See Geneviève Fraisse and Michelle Perrot, 'Orders and Liberties', in Geneviève Fraisse and Michelle Perrot (eds), *A History of Women in the West, Vol 4 Emerging Feminism from Revolution to World War*, The Belknap Press of Harvard University Press, Massachusetts, 1993, p. 11.
12. Dominique Godineau, 'Daughters of Liberty and Revolutionary Citizens', in Fraisse and Perrot, *ibid.*, pp. 15-32.

agreed that women were considered important and their opinions taken seriously. Husbands accepted their wives' observations and included them in decision-making.

Work became a publicly discussed issue as it never had before. As one historian puts it:

> The woman worker came into extraordinary prominence during the nineteenth century. She, of course, existed long before the advent of industrial capitalism, earning her keep as spinner, dressmaker, goldsmith, brewer, metal polisher, buttonmaker, lacemaker, nursemaid, dairymaid, or houseservant in the towns and countryside of Europe and America. But in the nineteenth century she was observed, described, and documented with unprecedented attention as contemporaries debated the suitability, morality, and even the legality of her wage-earning activities. The woman worker was a product of the industrial revolution, not so much because mechanization created jobs for her where none had existed before (although that surely was the case in some areas), but because she became a troubling and visible figure in the course of it.[13]

The 'problem' of the woman worker, as it is usually told, was that she was an anomaly in a world where wage labour and family responsibilities had each become full-time and spatially distinct jobs; before, she had been able to combine productive activity and childcare. This was not historically true, as we have seen; but the story itself was used during the nineteenth century to provide the legitimating terms and explanations which constructed the problem of the woman worker by minimizing continuities with the past, assuming the sameness of all women's experience, and stressing differences between women and men.

13. Joan W. Scott, 'The Woman Worker', in Fraisse and Perrot, *ibid.*, p. 399.

It also ignored the differences among men's work experience, which could also be interrupted and irregular; while there were some women who held permanent craft positions.

As we have seen, women's work before the industrial revolution was not all home-based industry combined with family care. Women sold goods at markets, were traders and itinerant peddlers, hired themselves out as casual labourers, nurses or laundresses, made pottery, silk, lace, clothing, metal goods and hardware, wove cloth and printed calico in workshops, and if necessary, sent their children to wet nurses or others. Most were young and single, working away from their own homes. Married women would have various locations of work, and the time spent on domestic tasks varied depending on the pressures of work and the economic circumstances.

This description is also true of the nineteenth century. The female workforce remained mostly young and single, in domestic service or textile manufacturing. Married women also worked in textile factories. There was no overall movement from work-at-home to work-away-from-home; it was from one kind of workplace to another. The textile industry was not the major employer of women; more worked in markets, shops, laundries, keeping boarding houses, and in making matches, artificial flowers, jewellery and clothing. Many women had a range of jobs. Needlework, always women's work, expanded as the clothing trades grew, providing steady employment for some women and a fall-back for others. Garment trades were many but poorly paid. Unlike factory jobs, much of the sewing industry work could be carried out at home, meaning that children need not be neglected in order for their parents to earn their bread.

A group who was relatively new to the labour force was middle-class women. With vast numbers of marriageable men killed in the wars of the early nineteenth century, there were many 'excess' single women, who now had to find ways of supporting themselves outside marriage. For the middle classes, social taboos made this difficult; most work for women was considered beneath them. Sheer numbers and need, however, forced change. And the need was great. As activist Josephine Butler wrote in 1868:

> The phrase 'to become a governess' is sometimes used as if it were a satisfactory outlet for any unsupported woman above the rank of housemaid. When we see advertisements in the newspapers, offering "a comfortable home", with no salary, as a sufficient reward for accomplishments of the most var-ied character, we sometimes wonder at the audacity of employers; but when we learn that such an advertisement, offering the situation of nursery governess, **unpaid**, was answered by **three hundred women**, our surprise has in it something of despair.
>
> The truth is, that the facts of the society have changed more rapidly than its conventions. Formerly muscles did the business of the world, and the weak were protected by the strong; now brains do the business of the world, and the weak are protected by law. The industrial disabilities of women, unavoidable under the earlier *régime*, have become cruel under the later. There is neither the old necessity of shelter, nor the old certainty of support. [14]

However Butler, close to feminist hearts in her efforts to gain working rights for single women, was anything but radical in her family values. A married woman herself, Butler saw her work for women's rights as motivated by regard for the family,

14. Josephine E. Butler (1828-1906), *The Education and Employment of Women*, T. Brakell, Liverpool, 1868. This can be found at: http://www.indiana.edu/~letrs/vwwp/butler/educ.html.

not as an escape from it.

Nineteenth-century women's rights movements worked to change expectations and opportunities for women's work, but not necessarily in opposition to family ideas. Women asked for equality of the sexes while insisting on their difference from men. In practical terms, activists were divided over which qualities mattered more in determining a woman's political status—the human ones or the female ones? Evangelical activists, such as Josephine Butler, argued that women were needed in public life because of their differences from men. Freethinker Mary Wollstonecraft, however, was opposed to the idea that women have specific virtues or belong in a specific sphere. The former representation steadily gained ground, and emphasized women's maternal capacities and the cultural contributions of women. The particular 'role of women' was used as the justification for educational and legislative reform. In this view, which remained dominant through the nineteenth century, the fundamental social unit was not considered to be the individual but the couple and the family.[15]

Conclusion

What has happened to families? In the late twentieth century, anti-family ideological movements have sought to redefine traditional ethics, particularly those involving sexual taboos and family arrangements. One would think that by now we could agree that this general movement has been a spectacular disaster. But ideology dies hard, and our society continues to

---

15. Anne-Marie Käppeli, 'Feminist Scenes', in Fraisse and Perrot, *ibid.*, pp. 482-514; Olive Banks, *Becoming a Feminist: The Social Origins of 'First Wave' Feminism*, Wheatsheaf Books, Brighton, 1986.

teach and believe that traditional families are artificial constructions of social oppression, particularly of women.

It is an argument that would come as a considerable surprise to the vast majority of men and women throughout the ages, as our brief survey has shown. Although selfish people abuse the structures, the structure itself keeps springing back time after time, as a remarkably stable and helpful way for people to live their lives. Marriage and family need not be oppressive, and even when they are, they have been consistently preferred to any other structure. In fact, marriage and family are frequently structures that bring comfort and protection to the vulnerable.

The astonishing thing is that, despite huge separations of distance and time, despite independent development and lack of contact, human societies have universally gravitated towards something resembling the biblical pattern of relating. People naturally want to live in family groups, with a father and a mother and children. In culture after culture we see monogamy upheld as an ideal, and taboos on anti-family behaviours such as incest, adultery and divorce. We also see pain, suffering and difficulty within families, and people treating each other poorly, but despite this potential for abuse, 'family' has been a solidly stable and remarkably tenacious social institution all over the world, for tens of thousands of years.

This is something about which there now exists a great deal of evidence. In general terms, the story is fairly repetitive until the twentieth century. That is, contrary to feminist and other twentieth-century re-tellings of the story, there is a mass of evidence that families based on the union of man and wife have been not just ubiquitous, but desired and *enjoyed* throughout human history.

These days, the ideal of the family is under threat, and we

will be looking at some of the developments that have so disturbed our society in the next few chapters. However, it is worth noting that at a more basic level the family is very strong. If we fight against it we will hurt ourselves, for the family is an essentially good and highly resilient structure. It takes a massive program of social engineering to destroy it, but we must be careful, for we now have the capacity for just such social engineering, through standardized education, mass communication and government policy.

The family is strong but it is not indestructible. And if we do succeed in destroying or severely damaging it as an institution, the result will inevitably be suffering, with the most vulnerable suffering the most—the teenage mothers, the fatherless children, the adults unable to find their sexual identity.

History demonstrates that the most stable and positive way to run a society is through families. Family has a tenacious shape in history, and this shape is completely consistent with the Bible's teaching about creation and relationships. The revisionist attempt to deny this needs to be seen for the ideological deception that it is.

— 3 —
Defining the family

We have looked at the history of families, and found that, on the whole, a remarkably coherent model of 'family' has survived for millennia, in any number of different cultures. Now we turn to what our culture understands as family today.

We find confusion. There has never been more research and study devoted to understanding marriage and family relationships, and there has never been more absolute bafflement about what it all means. More than that, there is a battle going on in academic and political circles about what a 'family' is. The details of the debate are very revealing; we are not dealing simply with observation, but with an ideological determination to reject certain traditional ideas, regardless of the cost.

In this chapter, we will look at the course of this debate, and see just how the battle lines are being drawn up.

What is a family?
What is a family? This is very difficult to say—or at least, that is what one would conclude after reading much of the academic literature on the topic. Although finding a definition for 'family' might seem a very basic, even self-evident, matter, modern commentators cannot seem to agree. Indeed, many have problems even with their own definitions.

There is some agreement, of course. Family has something to do with kin; that is, something to do with people related biologically. It also has something to do with people's chosen living arrangements. Apart from that, however, it seems very difficult for modern academia to say what 'family' is.

The theoretical approach

In 1984, a paper put forward three models of family policy:[1]

> The **patriarchal model** in which household and family are treated as synonymous or congruent, husband is equated with father, and income earner; mother is equated with wife and is responsible for household work and child care.

> The **equalitarian or egalitarian model** in which either the husband or wife are responsible for income earning, household work and child care. If they are sole parents, it is likely that they will be required to do all of this.

> The **emancipated model** which ... would show the following features:

> (1) Every adult is considered responsible for his or her own economic well-being. If a person is unable to support him or herself, the support would shift to the state, not a family member.

> (2) When an adult needs care, be it for permanent or temporary illness or handicap (including senility), it is the responsibility of the state (not a family member) to pay the costs of such care.

> (3) The cost for raising children is shared by father, mother

1. Margrit Eichler, 'The familism-individualism flip flop and its implications for economic and welfare policies', *Social Change and Family Policies: Key Papers*, AIFS Melbourne, 1984, pp. 431-676. Cited in Wendy Weeks, 'The Meaning of 'Family' and 'Individual' in Selected Social Policies: revisiting assumptions about age, gender and parental obligation', presented at *Family Futures: Issues in Research and Policy*, 7th Australian Institute of Family Studies Conference, Sydney, 24-26 July 2000. See http://www.aifs.org.au/ institute/afrc7/weeks.html. All family papers cited here are available on the Australian Institute of Family Studies website, www.AIFS.org.au.

and the state, irrespective of the marital status of the parents.[2]

Of the above three models, it seems that the first is the 'bad old days', which we are now escaping from, and the second is what has largely replaced it over the past 30 years or so. In 2004, social policy appears to be approaching the 'ideal type' of option 3 described above. But it seems we are even further away from agreeing what the family is, let alone how best to help it.

Part of the problem is that official statistics from bodies such as the Australian Bureau of Statistics, which are most frequently used when talking about the numbers of families in Australia, refer to 'household families'—that is, two or more related people who usually live together in the same household. They do not refer to families as people usually define them—that is, a group of people related by blood and/or strong emotional ties irrespective of where they live.[3]

The Australian Bureau of Statistics does not even attempt to find a single definition that will suit the one word, 'family'. Instead, it provides definitions of a number of different sorts of 'families', which are presumably all variations on the one basic thing, but without defining what that thing is:

Family: Two or more persons, one of whom is aged 15 years and over, who are related by blood, marriage (registered or de facto), adoption, step or fostering; and who are usually resident in the same household.

Couple family: A family based on two persons who are in a registered or de facto marriage and who are usually resident

2. Cited in Weeks , *ibid.*, p. 3.
3. Robyn Hartley and Peter McDonald, 'The Many Faces of Families: Diversity among Australian Families and its Implications', *Family Matters*, no. 37, April 1994, pp. 6-12. See http://www.aifs.org.au/institute/pubs/fm1/fm37rh.html.

in the same household. A couple family without children may have other relatives, such as ancestors, present. A couple family with children may have adult children and/or other relatives present.

Blended family: A couple family containing two or more children, of whom at least one is the natural child of both members of the couple, and at least one is the stepchild of either member of the couple.

One-parent family: A family consisting of a lone parent with at least one dependent or non-dependent child (regardless of age) who is also usually resident in the household. The family may also include any number of other dependent children, non-dependent children and other related individuals.

Other family: A family of related individuals residing in the same household. These individuals do not form a couple or parent-child relationship with any other person in the household and are not attached to a couple or one-parent family in the household. For example, a household consisting of a brother and sister only.

Step family: A couple family containing one or more children, at least one of whom is the stepchild of either member of the couple and none of whom is the natural or foster child of both members of the couple.

Intact family: A couple family containing at least one child who is the natural or foster child of both members of the couple, and no child who is the stepchild of either member of the couple.[4]

---

4. Australian Bureau of Statistics, 'Australian Social Trends: Family and Community – Living arrangements: Changing families', *Australia Now: 2. Australian Social Trends 2003*. See http://www.abs.gov.au/Ausstats/abs%40.nsf/94713ad445ff1425ca25682000192af2/ea563423fdbffd30ca256d39001bc33c!OpenDocument.

These broad definitions notwithstanding, it is widely felt by writers that extended family must somehow be included. For instance, Lois O'Donoghue, former ATSIC Chairperson, distinguishes her aboriginal culture's definition of family from the 'Western' nuclear definition:

> By 'family' I mean the various arrangements people make to ensure that the young are nurtured and people looked after. I am not restricting myself to the traditional nuclear family. The extended family is very important in Aboriginal society.[5]

Lois O'Donoghue has said during an interview that she remembers meeting her mother as an adult: "I learnt what kinship means to Aboriginal people—how in traditional society everyone has a place and a relationship with all other members of the group—the family. These relationships help ensure that everyone is looked after".[6]

Extended family relationships are very important. Unfortunately, they are difficult to limit, and so when social services and, more particularly, funding for them is in question, it is difficult for extended family to find a place.

Gail Bateman, for instance, in a paper entitled 'Defining Families for Policy Making',[7] asserts that the definition of family cannot be limited to two parents, two children, one breadwinner. This she puts down to "the changes in social structures over the last few decades",[8] although one wonders if families could ever have been limited in this way. But certainly

5. Lois O'Donoghue, 'Aboriginal families and ATSIC', *Family Matters*, no. 35, August 1993, pp. 14-15. See http://www.aifs.gov.au/institute/pubs/fm1/fm35lo.html.
6. Appended to the above paper.
7. Gail Bateman, 'Defining Families for Policy Making', presented at *Family Research: Pathways to Policy*, 5th Australian Institute of Family Studies Conference, Brisbane, 27-29 November 1996. See http://www.aifs.gov.au/institute/afrcpapers/bateman.html.
8. *ibid.*

now more than ever, given the great need for family services, the definition needs to be more flexible.

In that case, is a definition necessary—or possible—at all? Bateman is uncertain on this point.

> This paper is titled 'Defining families for policy'. At this point I think it is useful to draw the distinction between 'describing' families which allows flexibility and 'defining' which by its very nature sets boundaries of inclusion and exclusion.[9]

But, as she admits, "A major difficulty for Government is the resource implications of adopting a broader description of family".[10] Most Government benefits are based on very strict guidelines as to whom is allowed to benefit. But to a large extent, these guidelines reflect Government priorities rather than a consistent view of family structure. Bateman points out the inequalities that can result from this: for instance, when dependent students are defined as up to 18 years or 25 years for different tax purposes. It can also mean unjust inflexibility in providing government services.

> This is seen most poignantly in aged care where couples who after 50 or 60 years together are in danger of being separated between hostel and nursing home care, if their levels of frailty and need for care are different.[11]

Most people, Western or not, would probably agree with this idea at the very least: that 'kinship' creates a special relationship amongst people that is stronger than mere proximity of living, or even history together. Moreover, this kinship means that people are cared for. It is reminiscent of the old cliché,

9. *ibid.*
10. *ibid.*
11. *ibid.*

'Family is the place that always has to take you in'.

This is all very well. But when we try to be more specific, the vague ideas of 'kin' and 'caring' are not quite enough. And we do need to be specific, precisely because families are increasingly embattled entities. When families break up, or when there is disagreement over family rights and responsibilities—when the 'kin' fail in their general ideal of 'care'—the law intervenes, in an attempt to determine fairly and objectively what should be done. This becomes a very, very complex matter.

Jacqueline Campbell, a family law specialist, puts it this way:

> The definition of a 'parent' was fairly simple 30 years ago. Children's legal parents were almost always their full biological parents. They were usually a heterosexual legally married couple. In a relatively short period, the term 'parent' has become an uncertain and complicated concept.[12]

The freedom that people have now to organize their lives outside traditional patterns has caused problems not just for legal definitions, but for those most vulnerable in family disputes —the children.

> As a community we need to find adequate definitions for 'father', 'mother' and parent. We need to develop a model to respond to changes in the way children and families are created. If not, more children will be born into uncertainty and litigation about which adults are their parents. It seems a very basic right for a child to know who the community considers to be his or her parents.[13]

12. Jacqueline Campbell, 'Stepping forward or staggering about? Finding a definition of "parent"', presented at *Steps forward for families: research, practice and policy*, 8th Australian Institute of Family Studies Conference, Melbourne, 12-14 February, 2003, p. 2. See http://www.aifs.gov.au/institute/afrc8/campbell.pdf.
13. *ibid.*, p. 9.

Another logistical problem that arises is that if we include extended family in a definition of 'family', we do not know how to count them. This may seem a foolish objection, but in an age when policy and government depends on numbers and the ability to quantify, being able to count people is essential.

> The concept of the family beyond the household is outside the scope of censuses. Hence the household becomes the dominant group unit in statistical reports. As the domestic group or household is the major purchasing unit in the society, the image of family generally conveyed through marketing is also that of the household family. Thus, based on what is easily observed and measured, there is a strong tendency to equate family with household and to ignore the family beyond the household.[14]

Nonetheless, it is recognized that without an adequate understanding of family, society cannot prosper, no matter how economically vibrant it may be. Scholar Kevin Andrews, for instance, writes:

> It is a peculiarity of the modern era that national debate has been framed, almost exclusively, in economic terms, ignoring the social, the cultural, indeed, the spiritual dimensions of national life. There are three bases to a just and healthy society—a vital market, an efficient and caring state, and a vibrant community.[15]

Without community, democracy cannot be sustained, Andrews argues. Such systems depend ultimately on personal

---

14. Peter McDonald, 'Extended Family in Australia: The Family Beyond the Household', *Family Matters*, no. 32, August 1992, pp. 4-9. See http://www.aifs.org.au/institute/pubs/fm1/fm32pm.html.
15. Kevin Andrews, 'Developing a National Family Policy', *Family Matters*, no. 54 Spring/Summer 1999, p. 48. See http://www.aifs.org.au/institute/pubs/fm/fm54ka.html.

virtue and on a willingness to recognise the rights and needs of others, the very things that make a community. We challenge basic community structures at our own risk.

> In other words, if we cannot preserve and support the institutions of community in which relationships are developed and nurtured, then we are not merely placing at risk the welfare of many people, particularly the young and the elderly, we are weakening the very foundations of democracy itself. Of all political systems, democracy most depends upon the competence and character of its citizens. A liberal democracy presupposes civic virtue to a higher degree than any other form of government.[16]

Family fragmentation, Andrews argues, is threatening civic virtue. We need to find an answer. Unfortunately, if we leave it to theorists to come to an agreement, we may be waiting for this answer for a very long time.

The democratic approach

Many writers, then, have recognized that there are basic problems with trying to define 'family', but that it is vitally important for our society's health that we understand and help families. If we can't agree in theory, then, perhaps we can build up a model by surveying real families and trying to find a common ground.

This is a very labour-intensive approach, and faces significant practical problems. Nevertheless, just such a study was undertaken by Jenni Ibrahim, Principal Research Officer, Family and Children's Policy Office, Western Australia. She introduced her study by defending this method of studying the issue.

16. *ibid.*, p. 49.

Academic research doesn't always have a strong or direct influence on public policy development. And those of us working in government recognise how often public consultation forms a final rather than initial step in public policy development, after the policy direction and much of the detail has already been developed. Since the community is generally the major stakeholder in social policy, this seems a curious state of affairs.[17]

Individuals and families, she added, are also clear stakeholders in family policy making. "The very relationships which make them stakeholders in society help define the ways that human capital and an effective society can be secured."[18] For this reason, in Western Australia of recent years, state-wide consultation with families and children has been undertaken, in order to set the agenda for family policy in that state.

Some theorists argue that this form of research is misleading, since not everyone can be consulted, and in any case the very form of the questions and surveys reflects a theoretical understanding that will inescapably affect the data gathered. Ibrahim considered the research still worth doing. "[B]y taking a qualitative, rather than a quantitative approach, the actual words of families and children can more directly inform policy development ... The purpose of the policy research was to discover the views of families and children about ways to strengthen families, rather than to inform theory building about families or to measure family strengths."[19]

17. Jenni Ibrahim, 'Developing a Plan for Families: Listening to the Community', presented at *Family Futures: Issues in Research and Policy*, 7th Australian Institute of Family Studies Conference, Sydney, 24-26 July 2000, p. 2. See http://www.aifs.org.au/institute/afrc7/ibrahim2.html.
18. *ibid.*
19. *ibid.*, pp. 4-5.

A series of open ended questions were asked about what strengthened families, what strengthened families' links with their communities, and what government and business could do to be more family friendly.

The first challenge, Ibrahim wrote, was to engage as many families as possible, both by informing them about the consultation process and at the same time sending a message about the importance of families. "To ensure as inclusive a process as possible many alternative ways of participating were offered."[20] These included general community forums, special focus groups for different social groupings (aboriginal, new migrants, university students, homeless youth and other particular groups), individual responses sent in, and a talkback television forum.

By use of such diverse means of communication, a great many of the population could be directly consulted. The philosophy—that understanding of families comes best from the testimony of as many families and family members as possible—was thereby implemented. However, even with this effort, less than one percent of Western Australia's total population responded, which would seem to indicate an inherent weakness in this approach. Nonetheless, it was a serious effort to implement the idea of understanding families through community feedback. What were the findings?

Suggested ways to strengthen individual families were:

- value family relationships;
- promote male help-seeking and meet these service needs;
- prevent family breakdown (a small phrase for a large task!);
- stimulate early childhood learning in the home;
- provide services to help in a crisis;
- develop partnerships between school and family;

20. *ibid.*, p. 6.

- value the importance of fathers (we will discuss this further, later in this chapter);
- make the most of technology in children's learning; and
- provide preparation for fatherhood.

Various suggestions were made as to how links between family and community could be strengthened:

- be neighbourly;
- make it easier to get around;
- create lively supportive communities (again, easier said than done);
- address issues of job insecurity;
- respond to young people's needs;
- make it easier to balance work and family;
- provide safer home environments and child care at work; and
- improve community facilities.

One forum concluded that it was important to have a sense of community, which is "a connection of like minded people … Community gives a sense of belonging".[21]

> Young people's views were practical, positive and often went to the heart of the issue. For example, 15 year olds in a South-West town said:
>
> > What strengthens families is commitment, having a family pet, laughter and having fun, watching a sunrise together, having morals and rules to obey but not too strict, gossiping with your parents, teaching them modern day stuff. Kids need to know that they are loved in a family.[22]

21. *ibid.,* p. 9.
22. *ibid.*

70

These are all fine, practical suggestions. However, after all this research, the conclusions might be summed up by a statement from one of the community forums: "It doesn't matter how you define a family, what matters is good relationships".[23] This is the essence of the problem. We can try to decide what is good for people, but in the end if our ideas are based simply on gathering opinions from people, we cannot define what our most basic social structures are. As long as 'family' is just whatever anyone wants it to be, or even what a sizable group of people want to be, we have no basis for deciding what the best way of living is; and therefore we cannot put policies into place that will actually help people. Unless we have some agreed standard as to what constitutes a family, all we have are a mass of opinions, and no way of evaluating them.

The 'don't try' approach

Perhaps, then, the best idea is not to try to define family at all. For Robyn Hartley and Peter McDonald, the very act of definition would be unfair to 'modern' forms of family. It is imperative, in their view, to widen the definitions, so that members of families who might not have fitted an older norm "are less likely to feel alienated, guilty, or out of step, and they are likely to have an increased sense of wellbeing".[24] More than that, if we broaden the definition, "There is also a likelihood that the wellbeing of families in general will be enhanced, and parents and children will have broader and more flexible opportunities in life".[25]

That is, we must fight the discriminatory attitude that sees

23. *ibid.*, p. 8.
24. Hartley and McDonald, *op. cit.*
25. *ibid.*

71

separation and divorce as creating 'broken' homes. It is not long ago that:

> Children were automatically assumed to suffer long-lasting psychological damage, or worse still were ostracised, pitied, treated differently in schools, removed from their family networks or dealt with in various ways which frequently were far more damaging than the experience of their parents' separation or divorce. Many women who were sole-parents had to contend with punitive social attitudes as well as poverty.[26]

These attitudes lurk just below the surface, the authors contend: "there are still quite widespread differences in the way many people view widows (those women whose partners have died) as opposed to divorcees, separated women and women who have chosen single-parenthood".[27]

This is unfair, they go on, since the sole-parent family (for instance) is no new phenomenon.

> From the perspective of families with dependent children, in 1991, almost 17 per cent of these families were sole-parent families compared with about 9 per cent in 1971. On the other hand, the proportion of sole-parent families in 1991 was the same as it was in 1891, but last century the death of a parent was more often the cause than marriage breakdown. Thus, experience of sole-parent families is by no means only a modern-day phenomenon.[28]

These authors, then, are sure that there is *no* essential difference between single parenthood due to death, or single parenthood due to divorce or choice. There are many who argue strongly against this assumption. But for our purposes here,

26. *ibid.*
27. *ibid.*
28. *ibid.*

we may note that the debate over the definition of family is driven by this assumption, not actually by data.

A fundamental conflict

Nonetheless, the debate over defining family will not go away, probably for the very reason that families are so important to us. This was recognized by Don Edgar, long time Director of the Australian Institute for Family Studies, as he was retiring from the post in 1993.

> As Director of this Institute for the past 14 years, I have been at pains to emphasise that 'every individual has a family', that it is not just Mum, Dad and a few kids, that 'the family does not stop at the front door', that all families change over the life course, and that people define for themselves who is and is not part of their family. Children often include pets and unrelated adults when describing 'My Family'.
>
> But at the recent NSW Premier's Forum on Ageing I was puzzled by the unblinking acceptance of the term 'family of choice'. We were told that family is no longer limited by blood or kin relationships. Family is what we choose it to be, how we define it ourselves. And this can include friends living together, unrelated couples, a single person with a budgie, or a set of people not living together at all but who regard one another as family.[29]

For all that Edgar regarded diversity and the recognition of it as good, this seemed just too vague. He echoes many of the sentiments we have already observed in people's ideas of family.

---

29. Don Edgar, 'Parents at the core of family life', *Family Matters*, no. 36, December 1993, pp. 2-3. See http://www.aifs.org.au/institute/pubs/fm1/fm36de1.html.

Surely family is about blood and kin relationships, not about self-defined friendships that come and go? A couple of any sort may live together as family, sharing mutual care and responsibilities. They may even regard themselves as married, with all that implies. But without offspring or adopted children, 'the ties that bind' cease with the end of that relationship and 'the family' has no continuity through time.[30]

So family is more than just the people you live with, or the people you care for. An essential part of family, as Edgar sees it, is children; without being a basis for having and bringing up children, a group of people is not a family.

There is thus a problem or two with the notion of 'family of choice'. It may be adequate to describe modern adult relationships—we choose our partners, we choose whether or not (and when) to have children, we decide to separate, re-partner, form new families as we will. But children do not. Their family is not chosen, it is predetermined for them. It is defined in essence by who is called their 'parents' and they are usually inescapable. These groupings of children and adults have reciprocal family rights and obligations, not just socially constructed and imposed but inherent in the very relationship. 'Home is where, if you've got nowhere else to go, they have to take you in.' There is an emotional and moral attachment involved in such primary relationships that sets them apart from more rational, instrumental systems.[31]

But that "emotional and moral attachment" is the very thing that is so hard to pin down. For it cannot be separated from what people believe about marriage.

Edgar goes on to list many other changes in marriage and

30. *ibid.*
31. *ibid.*

family of recent years—changes in work patterns, working mothers, childcare and so on. These developments are part of what he views as a generally positive trend in society, as can be seen above by his reference to "more equal, more satisfying partnerships". Edgar approves of the ways in which family life is changing. But children still need parenting, and this is clashing with some of the changes in family functioning.

> International Year of the Family has to face the dilemmas of modern parenthood head on. It is not easy being a parent when most other institutions are still structured round the assumption that every child has at least one full-time parent at home. Children need close attention and we need new institutional arrangements to ensure their full development.[32]

What, then, do children need? Edgar goes on to list a number of basic requirements. Children are essentially conservative, he says; they need stability in their environments, not constant change. Children need security, a sense of being safe. Children need basic material resources and good community examples. They need time together with parents and family, and not just in front of the TV. Children also need a set of values and beliefs, Edgar writes.

> To feel part of something bigger than themselves is important for children. The ideologies of religion and politics may have their weaknesses, but they serve to embed people in a wider cause. How can we recapture that sense of being part of the civil society, where self-absorption is not the only ethic and where responsibility for others, a sense of being useful, of having a stake in what happens around us becomes the starting point for self-esteem?[33]

32. *ibid.*
33. *ibid.*

How indeed? How is this ideology of unselfishness and service of others to be recaptured? How are children going to get this amount of time, this connection with their parents? One thing is for sure—the modern academic community will in no way allow it to be through a return to those very philosophies that support such things. As Edgar has said elsewhere, the old ways must be rejected. The traditional family structure was patriarchal and (therefore) oppressive.

> That most basic shift of modern societies to an assertion of the equal rights of girls and women arises from the repressive structures of family life and demands a rethinking of the nature of family life.[34]

What kind of rethinking? According to Edgar, it must be a rethinking that rejects traditional ideas. "My point is simply that 'the family' cannot be treated as a static entity defined according to traditional structures or moral preferences."[35] Although he recognizes that children need certain basic structures in life—structures that, like it or not, traditional families supported—the old ideas simply cannot be accepted.

Edgar finishes this discussion with a very telling statement.

> The dilemma of our modern liberal democracies is that we defend our freedoms but are confused about the social and moral obligations that make that freedom possible in the first place.[36]

Quite.

34. Don Edgar, 'Conceptualising family life and family policies', *Family Matters,* no. 32, August 1992, pp. 28-37. See http://www.aifs.org.au/institute/pubs/fm1/fm32de3.html.
35. *ibid.*
36. *ibid.*

Defining fatherhood

One of the major problems in defining families has been defining fatherhood. From fathers historically being at the centre of the family, they have now been moved to the periphery, or done away with altogether. Fathers may still be necessary for procreation—for the time being—but whatever else they might be useful for is highly contentious. It seems that the answers to questions such as 'what is a father?' and 'what is his role in his child's life?', which were once self-evident, are now almost entirely mysterious. Should a father contribute to the development of children at all? There is a vague societal feeling that the answer should be 'yes'—or, at least, that he should contribute to housework and nappy-changing. But beyond providing basic labour in the drudgery of child-rearing, what do fathers actually *do*?

Richard Fletcher, Team Leader for the 'Engaging Fathers Project', Family Action Centre, The University of Newcastle, is one commentator who has done considerable research on this topic. The question of the role of the father is one which must be addressed, he says. In particular, it becomes vital when the very practical matter of providing family support is faced.

> When a mother is referred for post-natal depression, how much effort should be expended to include the father? When a boy is in trouble at school, should his dad be invited along? And if dad is now living interstate, should mum's boyfriend be contacted instead and should both men be invited to 'parents' night?[37]

37. Richard Fletcher, 'Defining fatherhood', presented at *Steps forward for families: research, practice and policy*, 8th Australian Institute of Family Studies Conference, Melbourne, 12-14 February 2003, p. 1. See http://www.aifs.org.au/institute/afrc8/fletcher.pdf.

The uncertainty about the role of the father, and the negative light in which feminist theory and discussion has placed fathers, has led to an unofficial exclusion of fathers from practical services.

> As a result … hospitals, schools, childcare centres and other bodies responsible for the welfare of children may treat fathers as either inconsequential or simply too 'difficult' to involve in the child's development, so that the father might find himself unaccountably sidelined, sometimes to the point of invisibility, and he himself may be left unsure of his role and identity.[38]

This is occurring despite the fact that more theoretical research is increasingly discovering a vital role for both parents in child development. Infants respond to secure attachments to adults; this is crucial not just in emotional development and coping skills, but for basic brain health and the development of neural pathways. It is known that wealth improves a child's chances of positive development, but fathers can provide more than financial security for their children. Interaction with a father can influence childhood cognitive growth.

However, beyond encouraging dad to do more housework, there seems to be a dearth of good advice for practical fatherhood.

> Although men's behaviours in family household settings are important in defining fathers' roles, we would argue that the way services, such as maternity wards, child care centres and schools relate to fathers is also strongly defining of fathers' identity … However, while progress has certainly been made, major obstacles remain. The female orientation of services addressing infants and children is well entrenched. It does not solely reside

38. *ibid.*, pp. 1-2.

in the attitudes, skills and knowledge of practitioners but informs the referral processes, procedures and policies surrounding service delivery. The difficulty is not that there is hostility toward fathers but that the invisibility of fathers is taken for granted. As one English survey of Family Centres found, many centres are 'agnostic' as to fathers: fathers' contribution to children is not the concern of the service. When services identify their target population as 'families' or 'children' or 'babies' it is accepted that mothers will be involved. 'Family' has come to be defined in the service delivery context as mothers and their children. 'Fathers' have come to be defined as irrelevant.[39]

No one, it seems, is confident to advocate any specific benefits that fathers might provide in child-raising. Fathers are ignored as non-essential; it is mothers who will solve children's problems, who are the child's representatives and advocates. As long as the role of the father remains so vague, it will inevitably be ignored.

Nor is this simply a matter of poor education amongst social service providers. This is a society-wide confusion that is reflected in law.

The confusion we observed among human services workers in deciding between a biological and a social conception of fatherhood is plainly reflected in the work of our Commonwealth and New South Wales legislators. What can be seen in the legislation is that different parts of the law describe fatherhood, differently. While there is a degree of consistency in the primacy given to biological indicators of fatherhood, in significant aspects of family law the social aspects of fathering are considered paramount. However, while recent changes clarify the importance of fathers in a

39. *ibid.*, pp. 3-4.

general sense, the legislation provides little guidance on the essential elements in the father-child relationship.[40]

It has become common for fathers' advocacy groups to complain about their unfair treatment in the Family Courts. One of the most common complaints is that while there is a mechanism for policing divorced fathers' payment of child support, there is no corresponding mechanism for enforcing 'access' visiting rights. Increasingly, fathers seem to be frustrated with their treatment, but without a return to the hated 'traditional' model, no one wants to suggest what a father's rights are. Neither are existing programmes designed to address this problem, Fletcher writes.

> However, with the exception of the Men and Family Relationships initiative of the Commonwealth Department of Family and Community Services, the strategies lack any recognition of fathers, assuming that targeting 'families' or 'parents' is adequate. The first step for those planning early intervention strategies is to recognise that fathers are not automatically included in family services and that including this 'other half' of the parenting population will require a significant reorientation of family related services.[41]

What is a father? What should he do? Sociological research suggests that fathers are valuable to children's development and mental health. On such grounds, Fletcher and others involved in fathers' advocacy argue that fathers should be more included in family policy and services. Yet what precisely are fathers to do? What should social workers counsel them to do? Do they have a role? Are they simply helpers for mum as she runs the family

40. *ibid.*, p. 4.
41. *ibid.*, p. 5.

and raises the kids? Is it enough for them to just hang around and pay the bills? With such vague and unsatisfying answers, it is no wonder that fathers are feeling left out. Imagine if a mother's role were described in such a way. Feminists have always fought against the invisibility of women—but the current invisibility of fathers is surely far too high a price to pay.

As a society, we are at a loss to define families, what they are and how they best function. Why this confusion? It is because received ideas, innate feeling (some would say these are the same), current ideology and trends in current legal and social practice are all warring against each other.

Is there any way out of this confusion? It seems we have, basically, two options.

We can accept that there is no real way to define 'family', and that people will do what they want to do. We can treat all living arrangements as equal under law and social acceptability. This is fair and non-discriminatory, and accepts a person's right of choice in personal relationship matters, and so follows the values treasured by contemporary Western society. The trouble is, this approach demonstrably leads to disaster in child-rearing and adult relationships. It also entails giving up the idea of 'family' as a coherent concept at all.

The other option is that we accept that there is such a thing as 'family', that it works, that it has been stable throughout history, and that it bears a striking resemblance to the Christian definition of it. We could accept, in other words, that the biblical story makes sense of what we all experience as 'family', and explains not only why it is so resilient as a structure, and so helpful for raising children, but also why it sometimes does not work, given the inherent selfishness of humanity.

Our social leaders and opinion-shapers, on the whole, do not seem to want this. Perhaps this is because it would entail having to accept: (a) that the Bible has something to say; (b) that the importance of fathers and the father's role taught in the Bible might be a necessary part of families working; and (c) that some relational/sexual behaviours are not acceptable. These consequences are ideological anathema to most modern secular commentary.

There is no middle choice. Either there is an absolute definition of family, or there is only opinion. If there is only opinion, we cannot legislate for or against particular conceptions of family; that would only be legislating prejudice. We can certainly argue that some forms of family have worse outcomes for children or adults, but such views have difficulty being heard. Consider the amount of evidence that exists demonstrating that children are far better off with married parents than de facto parents, and that the adult relationships themselves are stronger in marriage than in de facto situations. The evidence is there; but there is no social pressure, through legislation, lobbying, public discussion or any other forum to stop or even discourage de facto relationships. When there is no absolute standard by which to judge different social arrangements, people will always be able to argue that they have a right to the living arrangements that they want.

If we want to protect children and enjoy satisfying relationships, we must accept that this requires an absolutist definition of family. It is only ideological prejudice that is preventing us from accepting the strengths of the biblical model. We know that it works, and that it is a stable and successful social structure. We know that it provides the things that children and adults need in order to thrive. But we do not want to accept it. Our families pay the price.

Part II

CHALLENGES
TO FAMILY

We have now seen some of the confusion that current debates about 'family' face. There is no agreement as to what a family is, how we should decide what a family is, or what to do with suffering people in the meantime. How did we get into such a state of confusion?

Part of our problem is that certain modern movements have challenged the understanding of family that is taught in the Bible—which is the understanding that has framed the family structures of Western civilization. We are going to look at just three of these movements; in this chapter, the effect of reproductive technology; in the next two chapters, the pro-homosexual movement, and feminism. Each of these movements has been seen as a good thing in itself, and indeed there are positive results in society from some aspects of all of them. However, even though all three are intricately tied up with the notion of family, none has been sufficiently thought through with respect to how it affects family. In all three cases, our society has accepted a new movement through the activism of lobby groups unaccompanied by the caution that might have given time for more rational reflection. It is typical of our society that sound-bites and images are much more persuasive than rational argument. In the case of family, we will see just how dangerous that tendency is.

The three movements we are to consider all challenge the biblical idea of family, whether overtly or implicitly. Our modern reproductive technology separates biology from relationship. The pro-homosexual movement rejects the connection between gender and nature. Feminism asserts self-determination over relationship. All three, in different ways, seek to tear apart things that the biblical view wants to hold together. The result has been a fracturing not just of family as a concept, but also of many people's lives.

$\longrightarrow 4 \longleftarrow$
FAMILY IN THE AGE OF
REPRODUCTIVE TECHNOLOGY

In understanding what makes a family, we can probably agree that biology is not everything. A father who engenders a child but never meets it is not much of a father. On the other hand, the father who *does* bring up the child, a father by adoption, is much more a real father to the child. It is the relationship that makes fatherhood or motherhood real.

However, biology cannot be dismissed. The mother who gives birth to a child that is then given up for adoption, generally never forgets that child although she may never know it. Women who have abortions frequently know, years afterwards, how old their baby would be by that time. Adopted children frequently do want to know their birth parents. Biology does establish a relationship.

We see this most strongly, to our detriment, in the modern mess we have made of reproductive technology. With surrogacy and artificial insemination, a child can have any number of 'parents', and because any of them may have some legitimacy in feeling a bond with the child, the legal establishment has had to deal with a morass. And what a morass it is. If an infertile couple arrange for donor sperm to impregnate the wife's egg, and that egg is planted in the womb of a surrogate mother, who are the child's parents? Surrogate mothers, who carry and give birth to a child, feel like the child is theirs even if there is no biological link. When we separate reproduction from relationships, we create chaos; and because it is frequently done selfishly and with little appreciation of human nature and human sin, the chaos is very poorly dealt with. The possible advent of cloning only adds further confusion.

Vivienne Adair, a senior lecturer from the University of Auckland, has written of some of the problems that arise when families are 'assisted' by reproduction technology.[1] Until 1978, when the first in vitro fertilized (IVF) birth took place, the main option for infertile couples who wanted children was adoption. Now, with more single mothers keeping their babies, and a great many more babies being aborted, adoption has all but disappeared. Thirty years ago, nearly 10,000 children were placed with adoptive parents each year. In the financial year 1998-99, the figure was 544.[2]

The process of IVF tends to be emotionally and physiologically traumatic for women, and the success rate is relatively low. In the early years of the programme, the parents' own egg and sperm were used, so the children were biologically related to the parents. As the techniques have improved, the programme has been widened to use donor sperm, donor egg and donor embryo. In these cases the genetic relationship between children and their parents differs.

Along with this has come a shift in the legal definition of 'parent', which has created various problems. The couple who undergo IVF are the legal parents of the child born this way, regardless of where the gametes come from. Studies have

1. Vivienne Adair, 'Redefining family: issues in parenting assisted by reproduction technology', presented at *Changing families, challenging futures*, 6th Australian Institute of Family Studies Conference, Melbourne, 25-27 November 1998. See http://www. aifs.org.au/institute/afrc6papers/adair.html.
2. Susie Kelly, 'Adoption in Australia—an overview', presented at *Family Futures: Issues in Research and Policy*, 7th Australian Institute of Family Studies Conference, Sydney, 24-26 July 2000. See http://www.aifs.org.au/institute/afrc7/kellys.html.

shown that both parents and children are psychologically well-balanced as the children grow up—but for the vast majority who have been studied, parents have not told their children about their conception, especially where a donor was involved. Even those parents who say that they feel the child ought to know, and who may be quite open about the fact with other parents, still often keep it from the child.

These days, donors do not have the same legal protection to stay anonymous, and parents are generally encouraged to tell their children about donors, Vivienne Adair writes. But parents often worry that knowledge of a donor will harm the parenting relationship. Such issues are only likely to increase in complexity, as the technology becomes more widely available; now it is possible for surrogate mothers to carry embryos with no biological relationship to the eventual 'parents', or even to herself. What do the parents tell their children? The knowledge may, indeed, affect their relationship with the child—but then, so can secrecy. The question can be of vital importance to the child, particularly in adolescence when children typically deal with issues of self-identity.

So far, studies have shown various reactions in children who have been told about a donor parent. Many want information about the donor and may want to meet him or her. In studies conducted by Adair, all the donor-conceived children recommended that children be told the truth when they are young. Finding out as an adult has been shown to have traumatic effects.

The effect of being told somewhere between childhood and adulthood was reported by Adair in the case of a boy and a girl who were told at age 14 and 12 (a sister and brother). The boy said he was upset and angry when he was told because it had been kept a secret, and he would have preferred to have been told when he was much younger. He talked about it with friends because he wanted "to get it out and not keep it kept inside me".[3] His sister said she was "surprised, unsure about things, scared and cried because my brother was crying".[4] She said she wanted to know what the situation was because "If Dad wasn't my real Dad, then Nana wasn't my real Nana and Poppa wasn't my real Poppa".[5]

But just who is the 'real Dad'? As Adair points out, donors are not fathers by law and by choice. They do not parent a child and do not wish to do so. Until recently donors generally contracted to be anonymous, and recipient parents had no way of identifying donors. As more donor children grow up, however, attitudes to information are changing, as children demonstrate that they generally desire information about their genetic heritage. The effect of this on donors varies, too; one study of donors shows that they often do not tell other people that they have been donors, and that reactions can be negative once they do. Adair records a response from one man:

> When I was overseas I sat my sister-in-law down (my brother was away) and told her I had donor offspring. She was quite angry about it. "So you have placed this extra strain on us so if we produce a girl we have to vet her future partners. How do we do this? At what stage?" She thought I had been irresponsible (not my wife who had suggested it) and was quite vociferous about the way I had put upon them to check up on the relationships of her children even though they live in another country. My other two brothers were mildly amused and thought I had done 'a noble thing'. The youngest was quite brassed off because they have since had a daughter.

3. *ibid.*
4. *ibid.*
5. *ibid.*

They were annoyed because as they said, "We now have to deal with your problem because you had to bloody go off and have donor children".[6]

Another interesting result of this study was that previously it had been assumed that male donors would have no interest in knowing of, or meeting, offspring. For a significant minority, this turned out not to be true. Two comments from different donors:

> I was an anonymous donor but tagged possible change in the future. I was happy to have contact with recipient families or any approaches from children. If I personally was adopted or born as the result of a donation I'd want to know about my biological parents—I'd be upset psychologically if I couldn't have that information. So I'd be happy to give just what they wanted.
>
> I don't have any problems if a child wanted to meet me but I would want to know why they did. I guess it would be part of an identity crisis or something. As far as I am concerned donating sperm is no different from giving a kidney or blood. They might be curious to know what I look like, but my responsibility stops at that point. Having said that, in an extreme situation if a daughter of a family that was wiped out had to go into an orphanage I wouldn't refuse. But that is a humane thing to do.[7]

Evidently many of the donors were from 'care-related' professions such as teachers, welfare officers and police, and had seen the effect of neglect and abuse. As well, one of the contributing factors towards the decision to be a donor was the pleasure from their own children and those of their friends and family. They therefore had some interest in how the families were doing.

6. *ibid.*
7. *ibid.*

The first time I met the recipient parents I was enormously impressed. When you give donations you wonder what is going on in the family—you do wonder and wish for that child to have a good family situation. These parents are very level-headed, very responsible people. I have enormous confidence in them as parents who would bring children up in a very satisfactory way. They gave it a lot of thought.[8]

All of these reactions, although varied, demonstrate one thing: you cannot entirely separate biology from relationship. Both matter to people, in both directions—parent-child and child-parent. Sperm and ova are more than just body parts, as these reactions show.

So far, we have looked at fairly stable situations, where recipient parents raise their children within families, and donors are willing to concede rights to those parents. It can become much more messy than that. Jacqueline Campbell, a family law expert, surveys some of the real situations that have arisen from the technological possibility of separating sex from conception, and conception from upbringing. "Family law disputes about children are no longer just about the rights and responsibilities of parents and the rights of children. Courts may first have to determine a child's mother, father and parents. Biological parents may not be the social or functional parents or the legal parents."[9] The idea of just being a mother or a father has become much more complicated.

Imagine, for example, that a couple enters into a contract with a surrogate mother to bear a child which is not related

8. ibid.
9. Jacqueline Campbell, 'Stepping forward or staggering about? Finding a definition of "parent"', presented at Steps forward for families: research, practice and policy, 8th Australian Institute of Family Studies Conference, Melbourne, 12-14 February, 2003, pp. 2-3. See http://www.aifs.gov.au/institute/afrc8/campbell.pdf.

biologically either to the couple or to the surrogate (that is, using donor egg and donor sperm). If the couple were to separate before the child was born, who would the child's parent/s be? This is precisely what was at issue in a well-known Californian court case, *Re Buzzanca*.[10] Mr Buzzanca, the separated husband, insisted that there were no children from the marriage, and that he had no responsibility for the maintenance or support of the baby that was born. The first court in which the matter was heard essentially agreed, ruling that the child had no legal parents. The Supreme Court, however, subsequently overturned this decision. It ruled that the intention of the Buzzancas to have a child was the crucial factor, awarding custody of the child to Mrs Buzzanca, and requiring Mr Buzzanca to pay maintenance.

This is by no means the only legal case in which such issues have been thrashed out. *Re Evelyn*[11] was fought in Australian courts over the custody of a child born to a surrogate mother who was also the biological mother, with the sperm being donated by the husband of the childless couple. After 'Evelyn's' birth (not her real name), things at first went smoothly. She lived with her biological father and his wife (i.e. the intended parents), and their adopted son. After seven months, however, the surrogate (and biological) mother could no longer cope with the separation from her daughter, and removed Evelyn from the care of her intended parents. After various hearings, the court finally ruled that Evelyn should live with her biological (and surrogate) mother and her husband, along with her three half-siblings. The biological father and his wife were awarded visitation rights. Although the

---

10. 61 Cal. App. 4th 1410 (1998), cited in Campbell, *ibid.*, pp. 3-4.
11. 1998 FLC 92-807, cited in Campbell, *ibid.*, p. 4.

judge in the case denied that he had assumed any sort of priority for biological mothering in making his decision, observers saw the case as a 'win' for biological mothering, over both biological fathering and psychological parenting.

In general, in Australia and overseas, the parent is regarded as the person who rears the child. But there are many subtle variations. Terms used include: equitable parent, acknowledged father, putative father, presumed father, biological or natural parent, step-parent, alleged father, functional parent, birth mother, co-mother, co-father, co-parent, commissioning parent, collaborative parent, collaborative reproduction, psychological parent, social parent, intended parents and even biological progenitor.

In the midst of this confusion, what should the law do? It has been suggested that certain things should be absolute in law, such as a child's right to the truth about his or her biological parentage. As we have seen above, this is something children frequently want. The child's best interest is an overriding factor in most Western family law, but even that requires certain assumptions, such as the healthiness or otherwise of homosexual relationships. Is a child better off with its biological father who is in a homosexual relationship, or somewhere else?

In the case referred to above (*Re Buzzanca*), the Californian Court of Appeal made a telling statement:

> A child cannot be ignored. Even if all the means of artificial reproduction were outlawed with draconian criminal penalties visited on the doctors and parties involved, courts would still be called upon to decide who the lawful parents are and who ... is obligated to provide maintenance and support for the child. These cases will not go away ... Courts can continue to make decisions on an ad hoc basis without neces-

> sarily imposing some grand scheme ... Or, the Legislature can act to impose a broader order which, even though it might not be perfect on a case-by-case basis, would bring some predictability to those who seek to make use of artificial reproductive techniques.[12]

In a burst of scientific creativity, the second half of the twentieth century has seen relationship able to be divorced from biology. Carried away with our own cleverness, we have galloped down this route with abandon. The law is struggling to catch up. In general, hard cases should not define law; but it seems they always have in the matter of reproductive technology.

To what extent do humans have the right to control both their bodies and the embryos that can be created from their sex cells? Many of our ethical problems with reproductive technology arise from this assumption of rights. We assume, quite blithely in many cases, that we have the right to have children, or not have children, as we desire. Human history shows that when selfishness is allowed to reign, children are all too easily turned into commodities, to be traded, bought and sold or used up as we wish. The tendency has always been there, and still makes itself felt. But a frightening development has occurred; we can now control the very creation of children.

Advances in prenatal diagnostic techniques, such as genetic testing in the 1960s and 1970s, have made it possible to test a foetus (and more recently an embryo) for genetic diseases, such as sickle-cell anemia, and other disorders prior to birth. It is already widely accepted that parents have the right to decide if a sick child should be born. There is still some slight social squeamishness about 'designer' babies, but that is only

---

12. Cited in Campbell, *ibid.*, p. 9.

a matter of degree. We can already 'design' babies by elimi-
nating faulty ones; the ability to put together a bundle of positive traits is only a matter of further technical proficiency.
The right of adults to choose a healthy foetus over a faulty
one already exists. Why stop there?

Most parents who undergo IVF genuinely want to care for
a child, and want to be responsible parents. But the easier the
technology gets, the more scope there will be for children to
become commodities, to be ordered to specification. The
technology is not the problem; our own selfishness is. And we
underestimate our selfishness at our own peril. IVF separates
what God has united. God's purpose from the beginning was
that marriage, love, sex and procreation should belong
together. Marriage is a permanent covenant between one man
and one woman, which demands uncompromising faithfulness. But all forms of donation introduce a third party (the
donor) into this relationship. In the case of surrogacy, a physical and emotional bonding takes place between the 'mother'
and the child she is carrying, which may later be hard to break.

In an imperfect world, love, marriage, sex and procreation
cannot always be together—there will be widows and orphans,
infertility and adoption. But asserting a way of dealing with
children that ignores God's creational purposes will only end
up in a mess. Which is precisely what it has done.

What, then, are we saying? That IVF is wrong? That on no
account can we morally allow donor insemination?

That is not the conclusion I wish to draw; there is nothing
intrinsically wrong with either of these practices. There is,
however, something very wrong with the context in which
our society has allowed them to take place. We have blithely

gone ahead with the technology without sufficient thought for what makes a family. Too many simplistic assumptions have been made: that if you never meet the man who donated sperm for your conception, that he therefore has no connection to you; that as long as you grow up in a good home, it doesn't matter who your parents are, and so on. Time after time, we have assumed that we can separate biology from relationship with no consequences. We cannot.

We human beings have a general problem with technology: we think it can operate outside of a moral framework, that anything we can do is all right to do. But technology is a social issue, not a technical one. It always affects us in some way, and when it comes to tinkering with our most intimate relationships, the effects will have vast moral significance and greatly affect individuals.

This is not to say that reproductive technology in all its forms is a bad thing. Infertility is one of the greatest sorrows that can overcome a marriage, and the ability to rectify it is wonderful. It may even be instrumental in saving marriages. Our God-given ability to understand and manipulate the world and ourselves can be, literally, life-giving.

If only our moral maturity and good sense matched our cleverness. It does not; the Bible warns us that this will be the case, and from the very first book we have examples of humans using technology to demonstrate their own greatness without real concern about doing good.

We can create children; but children are not commodities. They will grow up wanting to know who they are, and can be deeply hurt by being torn from their biological roots. We cannot blithely separate the technicalities of manipulating human tissue from real relationships. We were made, in our physical bodies, to be in family relationships. It is no surprise to those who know their Bibles that major problems arise when we ignore that connection.

— 5 —
FAMILY AND SEXUALITY

Among those groups that have challenged traditional and biblical views of family over the past 20 years or so, none has been more vocal than the homosexual lobby. With campaigns to change laws to allow both gay marriage and gay adoption of children (or IVF), the homosexual community has tried to change the definition of 'family' to include same-sex couples and their offspring.

This radical reinterpretation of the concept of family deserves examination. Is it time for our society to update the definition of family to include gay families? What are the arguments for and against?

Homosexuality and society

It is understandable that those who consider themselves innately homosexual feel part of an isolated and persecuted minority. Homosexuality has been known throughout most of human history, but has almost always been marginalized, if not vilified and outlawed. In Western society, sexual acts between consenting adult males were decriminalized by the end of the 19th century in France, Spain, and Italy, but only much more recently in England and Australia. An incident in a New York bar in 1969 between the police and homosexual patrons saw the dawning of the Gay Liberation Movement. In 1978 the first Gay Mardi Gras was held in Australia, an event which came to be hailed as a cultural highlight of Sydney until its more recent financial collapse and reorganization.

The gay movement is now a social force to be reckoned with. Its proponents have been extremely politically adept. A great deal of energy has gone into public lobbying, through political channels and in the public media, and the major theme of this lobbying has been justice. After all, is it fair to *outlaw* acts that consenting adults do in private? Should they be called *criminals* because they prefer a certain kind of sexual stimulation?

The Western world has generally agreed with the homosexual lobby to this extent; homosexual acts are no longer criminal acts in most Western countries. Things become more muddied when we consider what the homosexual lobby has aimed for since then. It is clearly no longer enough for homosexuality to be regarded as not criminal; certainly it is not enough that homosexual persons be allowed to do what they wish in the privacy of their bedrooms. Now there is a push for the legal recognition of homosexuality as normal in a whole range of activities, including marriage, adoption of children and IVF. Schools are encouraged to teach not just that homosexual activity is allowable, but that it is good and should be explored.

One recent study of Australian school children expressed surprise and even dismay that a majority of students think homosexuality is unnatural.

> Boys, in particular, seemed to be particularly disturbed by the idea that any of their peers might be gay and the dominant feeling in the focus groups was one of fear. Part of the concern seemed to be based on the discourse that homosexual men are more predatory than heterosexual men. It may also be that boys are not used to the idea of being pursued in the way that girls are pursued by them. A senior student, a boy, expressed his concern in this way: "I'd shoot myself if

someone tried it. Like if I was drunk and some bloke took advantage of me and I found out, I'd kill them".

Fewer girls revealed themselves to be as staunchly homophobic as the boys and some girls were clearly exasperated with the attitudes of the boys. According to one senior girl: "[The boys are] pathetic. That's all they talk about. The main insult to each other is to say that that person is gay".

It is difficult to imagine the anxiety which must be felt by the young lesbian and gay students in the research sample. It is vital that school communities, and in particular educators, ensure that the needs of gay and lesbian students are acknowledged in sexuality education and life skills classes.[1]

The assumptions in this report demonstrate how far a prohomosexual viewpoint has been accepted. It is assumed firstly that there will be lesbian and gay students in the research sample, whether or not they identify themselves; and secondly that they need to be encouraged, rather than discouraged, in their homosexuality. The students who show a strong dislike of homosexual behaviour are assumed to be 'homophobic' and their views require re-education. In the same study, however, girls who expressed a dislike of sexual double standards and pressure from boyfriends to have sex, for instance, were considered justified in their dislike. There was no suggestion that they were in some sense 'sexophobic'.

Pro-homosexual moral assumptions appear regularly in public commentary. Recently *The Sydney Morning Herald* published the results of a survey in which 56% of those surveyed said it was reasonable to disapprove of male homosexu-

1.   Lynne Hillier, Deborah Warr and Ben Haste, 'The Rural Mural: Sexuality and Diversity in Rural Youth Research Report', National Centre in HIV Social Research: Program in Youth/General Population, Centre for the Study of Sexually Transmissible Diseases, Faculty of Health Sciences, La Trobe University, 1996.

ality. The editorial comment, however, was that the 56% of the population are therefore homophobic (a term which means having an unreasonable fear of homosexuals).[2] It is simply not possible, it seems, to express disapproval of homosexual activity without being irrationally afraid of it. No other kind of moral disapproval is given this treatment.

Just what is homosexuality?

The polemic of the homosexual lobby assumes, of course, that there is a condition or state called 'homosexuality'. Homosexuality is defined as something that you *are*. In popular discourse, you either *are* gay or you are not, although you may resist or deny the reality of your gayness for various social reasons. The assumption is that 'being gay' is not something you *choose to be*, and certainly not just how you *choose to act*. This assumption itself deserves investigation.

Most healthy people have sexual feelings. They can be aroused by all sorts of stimuli. How people choose to act on these feelings, what feels most satisfying to them, and what kind of cultural subgroup they feel most comfortable with, are all different questions. Of recent years, it has been politically popular to assert that gays are 'born'—that there is something innate and genetic about being homosexual that the person cannot help and cannot change. This is very contentious scientifically, and even leading gay activists have recently accepted that at least some gay people *can* change their sexual tendencies.[3] Certainly nurture must be allowed

2. Michael Pelly, 'Adultery's a sin but a little prejudice on the side is only human', *Sydney Morning Herald*, 4 May 2004, p. 3.
3. Simon LeVay, 'Can gays become straight?', *New Scientist*, no. 2416, 11 October 2003, p. 19.

some role in the matter. Researchers at QUT and the Queensland Institute of Medical Research, to name just one study amongst hundreds, have found that homosexuality is as much determined by society and environment as it is by genetics.[4] The more we find out about genetics the more we realize that this must be so—genes interact with the environment in highly complicated ways in order to produce any human trait.

This is not to say that all active gays have consciously chosen their leaning. Most report that they did not *choose* to be gay; they simply grew up feeling that way, and even if they struggled against same-sex attraction, could not necessarily stop it. However, to say that we experience consistent feelings in a particular direction is different from saying that same-sex attraction is 'hard-wired'. Many influences in childhood and community life can affect a person's development, and incline them to one kind of behaviour rather than another—even in something so personal as sexual attraction. We are the products of our upbringings as well as our genetics, and we are more than either.[5]

The more important philosophical point is whether it matters. All sorts of human behaviours probably have at least some genetic component. Violent tempers can run in families; so can musical ability or passionate natures. How one chooses to act is a different question. Humans have the ability to think about their actions, and the moral consequences of those actions, and to decide what to do. If an activity is wrong or harmful, then how you feel about it may not be

---

4. Carmen Myler, 'Homosexuality result of nature and nurture: study', *Inside QUT*, no. 169, 7-20 October 1997, p. 3.
5. For personal accounts of how it feels to be gay, see Christopher Keane (ed.), *What some of you were*, Matthias Media, Sydney, 2003.

relevant. Murder is wrong, even if you feel that you very much want to murder someone. Generosity and kindness are right and good, even if you very much do not feel like being generous or kind to this particular person at this time. In this sense, it does not matter if you are genetically predisposed to want to express your sexual feelings to a person of the same sex. What matters is whether that action is right or not.

Another misunderstanding about homosexuality is the way in which the popular media tend to speak of it as if it a were single recognized state, or movement. Even defining it by the homosexual community's own literature can be tricky. For different political purposes, various groups might band together, even though within themselves they are regarded as quite different. Being a cross-dresser, for instance, may be entirely different in feelings, lifestyle and social reality from being homosexual. Lesbians have a very different culture from gay men. They may all march together in a 'gay rights' parade, but that is not to say they are all the same cultural phenomenon.

Lesbianism, for instance, has been through many phases, and its nature is still a matter of considerable discussion within the feminist academic community. For many lesbians, from the beginning of the feminist movement onwards, it is impossible to be feminist without being lesbian. As long as one has heterosexual relationships, one is literally sleeping with the enemy. Lesbianism, then, is primarily about resistance to male domination; a woman's actual sexual activity, as long as it does not involve men, is a secondary matter. Adrienne Rich, in the paper 'Compulsory Heterosexuality and Lesbian Existence', suggests that genital sexual relations or sexual attractions between women are neither necessary nor sufficient conditions for someone to be thought a lesbian in the full sense of the term. Lesbian history is "woman–identified experience; not simply the fact that a woman has had or consciously desired genital sexual experience with another woman".[6] Even if writers do not go that far, they may well reject bisexual women from lesbian experience.

Consider this definition of lesbianism:

> Basically, heterosexuality means men first. That's what it's all about. It assumes that every woman is heterosexual; that every woman is defined by and is the property of men. Her body, her services, her children belong to men. If you don't accept that definition, you're a queer—no matter who you sleep with.[7]

'Queer theory', however, paradoxically asserts that there is no such thing as an essential sexual nature.

> Feminists developing a 'queer theory' perspective challenge both dominant and most dissident accounts of identity by asserting that sexual identity cannot be viewed as fixed, either in the sense of the self or in relational/hierarchical terms which establish set binary oppositions.[8]

That is, it is impossible to define a person by their sexuality; it is wrong to say that a person 'is' homosexual or 'is' heterosexual.

Sexuality, creation and the family

This brings us to a fundamental philosophical issue. Just how are we to know what it is to 'be' something—human, male, female, homo- or heterosexual? How do we determine such things? 'From observation' is the most commonsense and

---

6. Quoted in Ann Ferguson, 'Patriarchy, sexual identity and the sexual revolution', *Signs*, 7:1, 1981, pp. 158-172.
7. Charlotte Bunch, 'Not for lesbians only', in *Building Feminist Theory: Essays from Quest*, Longman, New York and London, 1981, p. 69.
8. Chris Beasley, *What is Feminism, Anyway?: Understanding contemporary Feminist Thought*, Allen & Unwin, Sydney, 1999, p. 97.

obvious answer. Humans are different from other animals. Males are different from females.

However it is not as simple as that. Some observable differences are superficial, and it is wrong to identify someone as fundamentally different because of them. Black people are not *essentially* different from white people, even though they look different. Feminism has always stridently insisted that biology is not destiny—differences in reproductive anatomy are not *essential* differences. Women and men are still the same in the ways that matter. So how do we decide what are the ways that matter? How do we decide which differences are worth recognizing, and which are not?

The decision that human societies have made almost universally throughout history is that the distinction between male and female is an essential difference rather than a peripheral one—that the obvious differences between male and female are both natural and significant, and that these differences form the basis of human sexuality and family relationships.

Speaking biblically, this is how God has created us. These basic gender differences, and their expression in marriage and family relationships, are a fundamental part of the order of creation, of the 'way things are' in our world. It is not surprising, from the Bible's point of view, that most human cultures have agreed with the rather obvious truth of this, and have developed remarkably similar structures of marriage and family.

However, what if a culture, or a segment of the culture, does not agree? What if they regard the differences between sexes as minor rather than significant, and socially determined rather than creational/essential?

This is the situation in which we find ourselves in modern Western society. The gay lobby is insistent that although homosexual behaviour occurs in a rather small minority of the population, it is nevertheless perfectly natural and normal, like left-handedness, and should be no barrier to setting up families or having full access to all legal and medical services available to heterosexual couples (such as IVF, in the case of lesbian couples).

It is an argument that many people today find persuasive. Surely, in a tolerant society, we shouldn't divide consensual sexual activity into 'acceptable' and 'unacceptable'. If two people of the same sex wish to pursue an intimate relationship together, why should we stop them? And why should our definition of 'marriage', and thus of 'family', exclude these same sex couples?

Leaving the 'God' argument to one side for the moment, there are two responses we could make to the gay lobby's position.

The first is to ask whether they want an *expansion* of the definition of what constitutes an 'eligible couple', for the purposes of legal rights and IVF, or an *abolition* of the definition? For example, take a pair of ageing sisters, who are not lesbians but simply live together companionably. The sisters are starting to get past marriageable age, and wish to bring a child into their household, either by birth or adoption. Since they are not married, in law or de facto, would they still be eligible for all the same rights as a heterosexual couple or a homosexual couple? If not, then they could quite reasonably ask, 'why not?' If the definition of family can be expanded to include gay couples who do not have reproductive sex, then why cannot it also include a couple with a loving and stable relationship (the two sisters), who also do not have reproductive sex? The gay lobby would seem to have no logical basis for arguing against this further expansion of the definition of an 'eligible couple'. But why should the limit be set at a couple? What if there were three sisters? Or three sisters, and a male friend who lived with them? Or any group of two or more people who had some form of friendship or relationship and who wished to bring a child into their household? It is hard to see how the gay lobby could say 'No' to any of these proposals, given the logic of their position—that is, that the traditional definition of family as 'husband and wife plus kids' is only one cultural construction, and should not form the basis of discrimination against those who choose (for whatever reason) to form different kinds of 'families'. How could they ask that the definition be expanded to include them, but then closed off so as to exclude others?

In other words, the expansion of the definition on the basis that the gay lobby is arguing for it would very likely lead to the collapse of the definition, and to legal, medical and social chaos.

'Well quite', you may say, 'but it would never get that far. Not every group of two or more people would make suitable parents. Surely the interests of the child would dictate that some couples (or larger groups for that matter) would be deemed ineligible on other grounds (such as age or mental illness).'

That brings us to the second point. If the 'interests of the child' becomes a key criterion for assessing the suitability of couples for adoption or IVF, then gay and lesbian parenting does not have a strong future. Almost every study that is available on the topic, and there are many, shows that the (male) gay lifestyle is almost universally unstable and unhealthy, and represents anything but a suitable environment for the nurture of children.[9] Further, it has been shown that children suffer considerable psychological disadvantage if they are not exposed to both mothers and fathers in their early years.[10] This of course sometimes inevitably happens upon divorce or

9. See, for example, Thomas E. Schmidt, *Straight and Narrow? Compassion and clarity in the homosexuality debate*, IVP, Downers Grove, 1995; also Jeffrey Satinover, *Homosexuality and the politics of truth*, Hamewith Books, Grand Rapids, 1996.
10. *ibid.*

the death of a parent, but to plan for such damage, to legislate for such damage, such as with lesbian parenting, would seem unconscionable if the main criterion is the interests of the child.

The fact that it is demonstrably better for children to have both a male and a female parent is an odd piece of data, if the modern trends in thinking about family are to be believed. Why should that be the case? If there is no essential difference between men and women, and if two women should thus be able to raise a child equally as well as a woman and a man, why does the research consistently show that the presence of a father in a child's life is all but essential to healthy psychological development? Could it be yet another witness to the stubbornness of 'family' as a creational pattern of life, as a means of raising children that is 'meant' to be?

Of course, the word 'meant' implies purpose, and purpose can only exist in the presence of Someone who ascribes it. In a biblical world, with a good Creator, there is a purpose to things, and a tenacious shape to things, and this bears a striking resemblance to the world we see around us.

Those who would challenge this vision of the world must show not only that their alternative makes sense on its own terms, but that it leads to better outcomes. The case for gay and lesbian parenting fails on both counts.

☞6☜
THE FAMILY SINCE FEMINISM*

It's an all too familiar topic among the legions of single and successful heterosexual single women who call Sydney home: this city's unyielding bloke drought.[1]

But the youngsters today have moved on again. They live together but it is no act of defiance and no trial marriage. It's part convenience, part love, part sex. Young people seem cautious about relationships but passionate about 'finding themselves' or finding the right career. They are conditionally in love at 23 and still single at 28 or 30. They have years of tentative love-for-now relationships ahead of them.

The young women are fiercely independent; it's how we bring them up these days. Young men don't provide financial support and young women don't dream of living off a man even while living with him.[2]

The new research implies separated fathers are perpetually poor because they are hopeless cases, or economic casualties. But it could be some men don't find it worthwhile to work, or to increase their income, because working, or working harder, makes them no better off after they have paid the required level of child support. They face very high marginal tax rates.[3]

---

* For a more detailed discussion and critique of feminism, see the author's book The Essence of Feminism, Matthias Media, Sydney, 2000.

1. Andrew Hornery and Joel Gibson, 'SPIKE: Sex and our city', Sydney Morning Herald, 3 May 2004, p. 18.
2. Adele Horin, 'Romance and the me generation', Sydney Morning Herald, 10 April 2004, p. 29.
3. Adele Horin, 'Pity the poor kids of loser dads', Sydney Morning Herald, 27 March 2004, p. 43.

Double Bay doctor Anthony Joshua, 31, said his 93-year-old grandmother can't understand why he hasn't been snapped up. But: "We [have] become discerning consumers of romance rather than romantics. We know we can shop around for the best romance virtually indefinitely before making our purchase … We have so many choices and offers in our everyday lives that we don't value anything any more unless we have to work for it".[4]

Last financial year, there were 5.25 million men in the labour force and 4.2 million women (latest ABS Labor Force Study). Just a decade ago, about 94 per cent of men aged 25 to 54 were in the workforce compared with only 53 per cent of women. That 40 per cent differential has plunged to 17 per cent (90 per cent of men and 73 per cent of women). The change is especially pronounced for women aged 55 to 64, whose participation in the labour market has doubled from 20 per cent to 40 per cent in just 10 years.

Almost one in four Australian households with children under 15 are headed by only one parent, and overwhelmingly that parent is a woman. Women are now succumbing to more work-related health problems, especially stress. Research at the Royal Melbourne Institute of Technology shows that Australia has the second-longest working hours in the developed world. It comes as no surprise, then, that the longevity gap between men and women has begun to shrink.[5]

What these disparate quotations reveal is a society attempting to come to terms with personal relationships in a post-feminist world. It's now the world in which we live and move

4. Miranda Devine, 'In tangled web of modern dating, love is hard to find', *Sun Herald*, 28 March 2004, p. 15.
5. Paul Sheehan, 'Today's young women—the new men', *Sydney Morning Herald*, 12 April 2004, p. 17.

and have our being.

It is very common, these days, to see women as major characters in TV shows about high-powered careers. Lawyers, doctors, judges, police—most staple TV drama series have their share of powerful women as major characters. It is also quite common to have romance between characters as a sub-plot. And it is just as common for the relationship to break up again. If there is a baby, what happens? Nothing much—the mother keeps on with her high-powered career, with or without the relationship with the father, while the nanny keeps on looking after the baby at home. Who needs a dad? In TV-land—where our most powerful role-models and cultural stereotypes live—marriages don't last.

On *The Practice,* defence lawyers Lindsay and Bobby fell in love, married, had a baby, and split up over the course of a few seasons. In the same office, Eleanor eventually had a baby by artificial insemination, with little prospect ever of having a permanent relationship with a man. *Law and Order* has had a series of single women assistant-DAs, including a single mother. The police boss is a single mother. On *The Bill,* we have had relationships form and break up, and a number of the successful women on the force have children.

But how often do we see a mother in one of these careers who manages to stay happily married to her husband? Almost never. That's not surprising; the feminist ideal of a career is almost impossible to maintain alongside a vibrant relationship and children. It just doesn't work. But what is disappearing, in our public representations of ourselves, is not the career; it's the man. Women are determined to work, to compete successfully against men in the career stakes; giving that up in order to save the relationship is simply too high a cost.

For anyone aware of the history of feminism, it's no surprise that this is happening. Since the early twentieth century, feminism has insisted that the equality of women depends on economic equality. Simone de Beauvoir was one of the earliest to make this a specific part of a feminist manifesto, in *The Second Sex*.

> It is through gainful employment that woman has traversed most of the distance that separated her from the male; and nothing else can guarantee her liberty in practice. Once she ceases to be a parasite, the system based on her dependence crumbles; between her and the universe there is no longer any need for a masculine mediator.[6]

Part of this insistence, in the early days of feminism at least, was due to the very communist flavour of much feminist writing. The family, as it has always existed, was seen as a particular barrier to class freedom, especially by women. The ideal was for children to be raised collectively in creches, or otherwise supported by the state, so that adult men and women could be free to work, as he (or she) was able, and so contribute to the communist state.

> A world where men and women would be equal is easy to visualize, for that precisely is what the Soviet Revolution *promised*: women reared and trained exactly like men were to work under the same conditions and for the same wages... pregnancy leaves were to be paid for by the State, which would assume charge of the children, signifying not that they would be *taken away* from their parents, but that they would not be *abandoned* to them.[7]

6. Simone de Beauvoir, *The Second Sex*, trans. H. M. Parshley, Penguin Books, Harmondsworth, 1972 (French original 1949), p. 689.
7. *ibid.*, p. 734.

Not many societies ever managed to put this into practice. The most consistent example was probably the kibbutz in Israel—somewhat ironically, given the strong family focus of Judaism. However, here where the communal idea of parenting has been most fully implemented, the experiment has rather sadly failed.

> Israeli kibbutzim are rapidly dismantling their collective child care centers and returning children to live with their families—because both the families and the community established that even a limited disassociation of children from their parents at a tender age is unacceptable.[8]

In any case, although the communist ideal did not continue in mainstream feminism, the imperative for women to have paid careers did. Betty Friedan, a career journalist, took the idea and placed it in a capitalist setting with *The Feminine Mystique*. Her argument, based not on extensive sociological research as she claimed but on her own ideology for women, was that in order to be fulfilled and happy human beings, women should pursue paid careers. The money was essential; without the tangible economic reward, work was not worthwhile nor acknowledged by society as worthwhile (something certainly not true at the time, although it has since become so). Women needed paid careers.

Indeed, given the definition of equality that has always been held by feminism—that to be equal is to be the same—financial independence for women is, indeed, a prerequisite for equality. As long as women are financially dependent on

8. Amitai Etzioni, *The Spirit of Community*, Fontana Press, London, 1985, p. 59. Quoted in Bill Muhlenberg, 'Deconstructing the family', *kategoria: a critical review*, no. 25, 2002, pp. 18-19.

their husbands, they can never be equal in that sense, regardless of how they or their husbands feel about themselves and their relationship. The activism of nineteenth-century women was largely on a different basis, recognizing valid differences between men and women, and indeed arguing for women's rights on the *basis* of their difference and so their ability to contribute something new to public life. The equality-as-sameness view, however, which has dominated twentieth-century activism, shaped feminism as it developed in the sixties and seventies. It demanded that women have public, paid careers just like men's careers. Such a view must sit lightly towards marriage, since the career takes priority. Feminism went further than that, however; the campaign to eliminate marriage soon became an overt goal.

One of the most strident proponents of this view was Germaine Greer: "If women are to effect a significant amelioration in their condition it seems obvious that they must refuse to marry".[9] She is still against trying to pursue marriage, offering segregated households as a desirable alternative.

> More and more we are finding that matrilocal families including grandmother-figures and aunt-figures have established themselves from the fall-out of the nuclear family. Such segregated communities may hold great advantages for women and children.[10]

Given the ideological dominance of feminism in our society, it is no surprise that marriage and family are suffering. Even if feminism had not fought so strongly against marriage, the very fact that women are determined to, and now virtually

9. Germaine Greer, *The Female Eunuch*, Paladin, London, 1971, p. 319.
10. Germaine Greer, *The Whole Woman*, Alfred A. Knopf, New York, 1999, p. 342.

forced to, consider having full-time careers, must put intolerable stresses upon marriage.

This is the dilemma for modern women—they are urged to be independent and have a career, and yet the vast majority still yearn for a satisfying marriage relationship and children. And the two seem deeply incompatible.

There is one solution, of course, which is happening in the more affluent parts of society: the re-creation of a female servant class. Women really can have it all—careers, husbands and families—if full-time servants can be found to run the household and look after the children.

> With the arrival of a cheap, easily exploited army of poor and luckless women—fleeing famine, war, the worst kind of poverty, leaving behind their children to do it, facing the possibility of rape or death on the expensive and secret journey—one of the noblest tenets of second-wave feminism collapsed like a house of cards. The new immigrants were met at the docks not by a highly organized and politically powerful group of American women intent on bettering the lot of their sex but, rather, by an equally large army of educated professional-class women with booming careers who needed their children looked after and their houses cleaned. Any supposed equivocations about the moral justness of white women's employing dark-skinned women to do their s**t work simply evaporated.[11]

It is a fundamental betrayal of any kind of feminism, but at least it means the career can survive.

For the majority of women, however, life has been transformed for the worse, and the blatant reality of this fact is

11. Caitlin Flanagan, 'How Serfdom Saved the Women's Movement: Dispatches from the nanny wars', *The Atlantic Monthly*, March 2004, pp. 113-114.

only equalled in strength by the public censorship on saying so. Most women these days do not want full-time careers. A minority of women do, and many of those are willing to give up the notion of marriage and family to pursue careers. As *Time Magazine* puts it:

> Theresa M. Welbourne at the University of Michigan Business School studied stock value and earnings growth following initial public offerings in the U.S. and found that IPOs were significantly more successful when the companies involved had senior female executives. "Having women in the top management team results in higher earnings and greater shareholder wealth", she concluded. So why, in egalitarian havens like Norway and Sweden, haven't more women risen to positions of power in business? Could part of the explanation be that they don't want to?[12]

For the vast majority, *some* work is desired, since that is where normal adult interaction happens these days (most of the voluntary contexts in which this would have happened in the past having been dismantled). But many, many women are forced, either by societal pressure or finances or both, to work more than they want to. Family suffers when this happens. And when families suffer, the nation suffers. What, however, is the solution?

Governments are expected to come up with 'something'. The precise type of solution varies from party to party, but most agree that it is somehow the government's job to make this mess work. Socially conservative parties tend to favour family payments and tax incentives, enabling a woman to spend more time at home without facing financial sacrifice. In

12. Amanda Ripley, 'Equal Time', *Time Online Edition*, 14 September 2003, p. 2. See http://www.time.com/time/nation/article/0,8599,485708,00.html.

Australia, the Howard government has favoured this approach. It has come under strong criticism from feminists and others, partly because it just does not involve enough money—certainly it does not compete with working salaries. Feminist groups favour instead fully paid maternity leave, and other paid leave allowances which make parenting financially viable even when parents are at work rather than at home. The Swedish family policy is held up as ideal.

It is notable, however, that the Swedish family policy as advertised on a web page by the Ministry of Health and Social Affairs (23 September 2003) begins: "Swedish family policy is based on the principles of universality and individual rights".[13] Indeed. It is *not* based on principles of family rights, or family responsibilities, or anything to do with families at all. It is based on individuals—and the focus on individuals is one of the very problems that plague our family-hostile society.

There is another, perhaps more fundamental, issue raised by feminism that challenges the nature of family. Feminism is a movement that, above all, asserts that a woman should be independent. Whether this is expressed in a radical way, proposing radical lesbianism and the death of the male, or merely asserting that a woman should ensure her financial independence and self-determination apart from being a wife and mother, the issue is independence.

Feminism encourages women to aim for achievement; it appeals to every woman's desire for recognition and worth, but defines these things in terms of power and its con-stituents—money, fame, social status. The most successful

13. See http://www.sweden.se/templates/FactSheet____6952.asp.

women are those in charge of businesses, or in government, or in universities. The goal for women is to break the 'glass ceiling', to see equal numbers of women and men in the *powerful* positions. Feminism teaches women to get ahead by competing with and beating others. It tells women, above all, to have a 'career'—a telling word, that means 'race', as women are pushed to compete with men and each other for the top.

Self-sacrifice for the sake of others, contentment, identification with family and service of children—these things are not celebrated by feminism. Indeed, they are overtly opposed as the very things which 'held women back' for centuries. The fact that so many women *want* to follow such a path is merely social conditioning, brainwashing forced upon them by a patriarchal society. The idea that such goals might be good things, a worthwhile and satisfying way to live a life, is feminist heresy.

These words sound harsh in our feminist society. Surely, it might be objected, what feminists have chiefly argued for is *choice*? That women can look after children if they want to, but be free to choose a career if they wish? The problem is that the choices championed by feminism are all about self-determination. A woman should do what makes her feel most empowered. In the very unlikely event that looking after children does this, then yes, she may choose that; but this choice does not really fit into the feminist schema for life. It preaches success through achievement of visible goals; not success through loving relationships.

Consider the opinions of Anne Summers, a leading Australian feminist.

> The breeding creed aims to reverse, or at least arrest, that falling rate in fertility by making it difficult, even prohibitive, for women to have jobs, especially full-time jobs, and

have children. Since the late 1990s the Government has made ruthless use of child care, employment, family assistance and taxation policy to steer women with children out of the workforce and into full-time motherhood. It has, via Family Tax Benefit A and the Child Care Benefit, imposed substantial financial penalties on mothers who continue to work. The intention is, apparently, to make it financially attractive for women to become full-time mothers in the hope that this will encourage more women to have children, and for those who already have them, to have more.[14]

A budget that has made it easier for women to choose to stay at home means that it is comparatively harder for women to work. That's the nature of comparative terms; if one is easier, another is harder, even if it is still quite possible. But while the government doctrine which encourages family home-life emphasizes the 'easier to stay at home' side, feminist doctrine emphasizes the 'harder to have a career'. Feminism sees careers and professional work for women as intrinsically more valuable than caring for a family. Independence and power are the goals for a feminist life.

It is a doctrine doomed to failure, for no one is independent, and those who try are lonely and unsatisfied. The problem of the male 'mid-life crisis' has been recognized for years as a manifestation of this—that in the end, money, power and career do not satisfy. Indeed it is becoming more common for women, having entered and succeeded in the world of men, now to experience a kind of female mid-life crisis. Work just isn't as satisfying as it was made out to be. Career achievements, money, independence—is that all? There must be more

14. Anne Summers, 'Corralled back to the kids and kitchen', *Sydney Morning Herald*, 24 May 2004, p. 9.

to life than this. I have lots of *things*, but they don't satisfy. But relationships, sex, marriage and children don't necessarily satisfy either.

The problem is not in the achievements, but in the goal. Satisfaction, like happiness or fulfilment, eludes those who chase it. It is only ever a side-effect. We will stay miserable until we recognize that happiness is not a viable goal in life. We were not made for ourselves. It is not surprising, then, that when we try to live for ourselves, it doesn't work.

Happiness and fulfilment, as ends in themselves, are not worthwhile goals in life. Love (as in our love for others, not the feeling or experience of love), charity, honour, faithfulness—these are goals worth pursuing. It is a good goal to stay married not because it is still fulfilling or enjoyable, but because we promised to. We have and raise children not because of the joy and rewards involved, but because it is good for the children. We act not to benefit ourselves but because certain acts are right. In doing this, we are paradoxically much more likely to experience happiness. Actually, it is not a paradox when we understand that this is precisely what we were created for—to serve others. Living the way we were created to is in itself satisfying. It is no accident that Christian believers, who embrace the biblical worldview, are statistically the happiest in society.[15]

There will be social, structural and legislative change which can bring about more fairness in people's lives, which recognize the nature of a technological, wealthy society and how

15. Bob Holmes, Kurt Kleiner, Kate Douglas and Michael Bond, 'Reasons to be cheerful', *New Scientist,* no. 2415, 4 October 2003, p. 47.

people live in it. We can indeed enforce job-sharing, parent-friendly arrangements, the better allocation of profits, and so on. But it will not work without parents being committed to each other and to their children over and above career or money. It will not happen without parents accepting and approving a lifestyle of restraint instead of consumption.

The all-or-nothing approach to work is a major part of the problem. It is driven by greed—for money and for achievement. Work can be stimulating and interesting without being a career, and certainly without earning lots of money. But as long as parents have those two goals, no amount of childcare arrangements will save the family.

On the other hand, an all-or-nothing assumption about the at-home mother is also misleading. There is no evidence to demonstrate that a mother must *always* be with her children. There is no objection that I know of, biblical or otherwise, to mothers (or fathers) getting babysitters while they go out, for whatever reason. Most children seem to benefit from some days at childcare/preschool, the chance to play with other children, develop social skills, and have structured activities.

What is *not* beneficial is too few carers per child, long day care, frequent turnover of carers, untrained or irresponsible carers. Five days a week at long stay child care is too much.[16] But in our highly technological society, where work skills can be very far removed from the physical, and housework so largely mechanized, the demarcation of work along gender lines makes less and less sense. Mothers always worked; they

---

16. See, as one example amongst many studies, Peter S. Cook, *Early Child Care: Infants and Nations at Risk*, News Weekly Books, Melbourne, 1996. For a review of Cook's study, see Dani Scarratt, 'Handling children with care', *kategoria: a critical review*, no. 8, 1998, pp. 61-69.

just usually worked inside the home. But a mother doing the laundry is a mother doing the laundry, not a mother looking after the children; the fact that she's at home, or at least in the vicinity of the house, does not change the fact that she is working at something other than looking after the children.

Society and the kind of work we have to do in order to live has changed. But the expectations on mothers, and the social structures in place for mothers, have not. Must all the time mothers now have not doing the housework be spent looking after children? The old non-employed mother didn't spend all her time looking after the kids; the modern equivalent is not a stay-at home mum, but a part-time working mum. Mothers used to stay at home in order to do the housework, not just to look after the kids. The time now spent not doing house-work can be spent doing some other kind of (more interesting) work these days. That is, of course, if mothers can resist the challenge to be Mrs Perfect, and don't simply spend the extra time creating even more spotless polished floors.

But not only have we this all-or-nothing approach to women's work, we also have a vastly inflated idea of what children require. So if a mother wants to do interesting work, she's not only required to do far more hours of it than is healthy for the family, but she's also told to do far more for her child, so it grows up a prodigy in music, athletics, languages, art and culture as well as a super academic. It is no wonder that the burden of being a working mother is so impossible.

The burden is largely of our own creation; a result of selfishness, and the desire to have all possibilities at once, for parents as well as children. One of the big complaints that feminists have is that a man can have a family and career as well, but a woman actually takes on two full-time jobs when she does so. But let us consider that a little. A man has a good career, he gets married, and they start having children. Can the man continue his life once the children are born with no significant difference? Yes, if he never spends time looking after and doing things with his children. In other words, if he's a bad father. If, on the other hand, he has any interest in actually bringing up his children, his life will become much busier and more stressful—just like a woman's will.

There is a difference, of course, but it's not one of institutional discrimination. A father who cares about and for his family has exactly the same choice as his wife—to spend his time working for money, or time raising children. Men have generally chosen to spend the majority of their time in work, to care for their families by providing for them materially. Not every man does so, and it is not always a good decision; in a sinful world, this decision can easily be affected by ambition, greed, or capitulation to peer pressure. But it is generally how men want to care for their families.

Women, on the other hand, generally choose time with their children over time in paid outside work, if given the choice. Not always, and again it can be a decision forced by peer pressure. But by far the majority of women want to spend time looking after their children. It is *women* who have the problem of guilt feelings when they are away from their children, dropping them at childcare and having to say goodbye. This is not a widespread *male* problem, even amongst single fathers. It is not men who have books and TV shows telling them how to deal with their feelings of guilt. Men and women have the same choice between work and children— but it generally does not tear men the way it does women.

Feminism has given women a totally impractical picture of

what is possible. There are only twenty-four hours in the day for each of us. You *cannot* have two full-time jobs. If you have a full-time career, you will not be spending much time with family. If having the career tears you apart and leaves you ragged because you can't give up wanting to be a diligent mother and housekeeper as well, then give up the career. Or give up wanting to be a mother. But most women find that particular 'want' a very hard one to give up.

Fathers can have the same problem. A father who never gets to see his children awake during the week might feel considerably deprived and sad about that. He might feel guilty and that he's not meeting his family responsibilities, and even decide to take a less demanding job to spend time with the family. Or he might want to, but cannot afford to. Men have to make their choices and accept reality too.

Women have also been deceived to some extent about the value of a career. This is partly due to feminism, and partly due to the pervasive individualism and materialism of our culture. A career is held up as the path to fulfilment, and material goods the way to happiness. But no job is perfect. A professional career is not necessarily more exciting, more varied and interesting than raising children. Work also involves drudgery and boredom and lack of freedom. The high points of work—the satisfaction of achievement and peer recognition, the experience of social power and financial gain—are far more obvious, but not necessarily *better* than the high points of raising children. We are very tempted by obvious glamour, without recognizing either the downside of paid careers or the highs of family life.

Anne Wilkinson, 48, knew her career as a European Commission lawyer was on "skid row" when she decided to work part time in 1992 so she could take care of her four children. "There is an unwritten rule at the Commission that you simply do not get promoted if you work part time", she says. After taking a leave of absence in 1995, and returning to full-time work in 2002, she quit last month. She felt she was wasting her time. "I don't know many women who think it's an achievement to sit in an office and fly around the world for 80 hours a week", she says. "I think most women regard it as imbecilic." She says she has found a truer sense of achievement in raising her children: "That's where you have real power and influence over the future".[17]

We must also recognize that this debate is dominated by the wealthy. Most people in the world, even the Western world, have very little choice about how to spend their adult lives. It is only very recently in history that any but the most affluent have had this choice. For those of us in the middle-class Western world who do have choice, it has limited value. In fact, for many of us the wide options of choice simply tear us apart as we try to do everything. We don't just want choice, we want everything, and we want to ignore that some choices may be mutually exclusive.

A growing number of women are waking up to this truth—that they can't have everything. Because career is more immediately rewarding, and pushed socially as overwhelmingly good, vast numbers of women have 'chosen' career over children. Of course, many women are starting to recognize that the career may not be that great a choice. But that's the sort of thing you might not realize until it's too late; when you're trapped in a financial situation that needs the income, or just too conditioned to need the status of career to be able to give it up. There is as much pressure now for middle-class women to be educated and have a career as there ever was to

17. Amanda Ripley, *op. cit.*, p. 3.

stay at home with children.

But where does this philosophy and teaching come from? From the most task-oriented, career-hungry people in society; from the small percentage who are driven to succeed, for whom that dream of achievement is enough. We used to feel sorry for such people. 'Careerist' used to be an insult. Such people miss out on what life is really about. So why do we listen to their ideas on how to live?

Feminism has changed the face of our society. Many individual feminists may have had noble and altruistic goals, but the movement has not achieved those goals. It is no closer to doing so. Its effects have been to hurt families, and that includes all members of the family.

Any relationship requires an element of self-sacrifice. The most precious and close relationships—those within a family—require the most. In pursuing the good of one's family, a person is most likely to experience joy and happiness, for close relationships produce these things. One may also experience the greatest level of hurt and frustration. That is the risk. One does not come without the other.

The situation becomes infinitely more strained and risky, however, when goals of personal pride and power are forced upon either of the parents. It is bad for a family when a father pursues such goals; it is even worse when both parents do so. Feminism has not succeeded in persuading fathers to be less selfish; indeed, it did not try. On the contrary, it has been very successful in persuading mothers to be more selfish. In doing so, the traditional family structure has been strained to breaking point.

Is it good that mothers are stressed, unhappy and wracked with guilt? Is it good that fathers are confused, encouraged to be irresponsible and discarded as irrelevant? Of course not. As long as we idolize the career as the main goal of successful human beings, this is what we will get.

God does not forbid women to have careers; nor men. What he is against is self-centredness, because such behaviour is destructive of ourselves and others. What you do with your life, what career path you follow, is, according to the Bible, always secondary to how you consider other people. That is how to foster our most precious relationships. Ignoring God's vision of how to relate, in particular of how to relate in families, leads to precisely the mess we see now.

— 7 —
CONCLUSION

Families are important to us. They should be. Not only are they the single most stable social unit throughout history, but they are the places where we experience our crucial formative years and our closest emotional ties. It is a tragedy when family goes wrong, and that is happening far too often.

Our current society idolizes selfishness. Of course, humans have always been selfish, but our economic prosperity and scientific technology have enabled us to exercise selfishness in hitherto unprecedented ways. We have accepted an ideology that to serve oneself is right and desirable. If you feel like giving up family for career, then you should do it. If you feel sexually attracted to the same sex, then you should foster and realize those feelings. If you feel like having a child, have one. It's your right.

In this self-centred world, we are suffering the loss of relationship. People crave relationship, companionship, security and love, but these things do not come automatically. Until we are prepared to give up the creed of devotion to self, they will not be what characterizes our society. Some have given in, and accepted it; accepted that lifelong singleness punctuated by a few affairs is the best to hope for; that single parenthood may as well be the norm. Most continue to fight for things such as family and home, but without being prepared to give up their self-worship; it is time we realized that these two values together are impossible to hold.

Throughout this book, it has been argued that family goes

wrong when the biblical picture is ignored, or worse still, out-right rejected. Moreover, the Bible actually explains better than any other philosophy why it is that we crave and need family so much—as well as why we sabotage it with our selfishness.

Family is a good thing. It is what we were created for. It is not the ultimate value; it is not the source of heaven on earth. It is, however, the best way to live, because that is how we were made to live. Ideology will not change that. And if we continue to fight against family structures, we will continue to suffer.

The defence of family is a matter of common sense above anything else. It is not homophobia, or a yearning for white picket fences. It is not slavery of women, or a return to the fifties. All those reactions are wildly inappropriate. What this book has argued is that we are made for a certain way of relat-ing. History bears this out; our recent attempts to go against it have led to disaster; without it we find a very confused debate with nowhere to go. Hard as it may be to admit, it makes sense to accept what the Bible has been saying all along.

This is not to say that the Bible is 'fanatical' about family values. It is actually about salvation, about how to escape this world of death where even good things like families are per-verted and can lead to suffering. That is what is most impor-tant in this life. However, Christians are also generally concerned to help others, and promoting a good and healthy way to live—such as in family life—is one way to help others. Those who promote the rejection of family structures are not helping others. It is as simple as that.

Should the government enforce a biblical model of family? Of course not—unless we want some kind of police state. Relationships cannot be legislated. Laws will not change peo-ple's hearts. However it is foolish for governments to actively oppose a biblical model of family, when it demonstrably works so well for so many people. In so far as family is a matter for law, it is right for the law to support the model that works best for the most people.

God knows best. This is a message that it is always hard for wilful humans to hear. But it does not change the truth.

matthiasmedia

Matthias Media is an independent, evangelical, non-denominational company based in Sydney, Australia. We produce an extensive range of Bible studies, books Bible reading materials, evangelistic tools, training resources, periodicals and multimedia resources. In all that we do, our mission is:

To serve our Lord Jesus Christ, and the growth of his gospel in Australia and the world, by producing and delivering high quality, Bible-based resources.

For more information about our resources, and to browse our online catalogue, visit our website:

www.matthiasmedia.com.au

US customers may visit www.matthiasmedia.com.

In the UK and Europe, our resources are distributed by The Good Book Compan Visit their website at www.thegoodbook.co.uk.

You can also contact us in any of the following ways:

Mail:	Matthias Media PO Box 225 Kingsford NSW 2032 Australia
Telephone:	1800 814 360 *(tollfree in Australia)* 9663 1478 *(in Sydney)* +61 2 9663 1478 *(international)*
Facsimile:	9663 3265 *(in Sydney)* +61 2 9663 3265 *(international)*
Email:	info@matthiasmedia.com.au

The Essence of Feminism

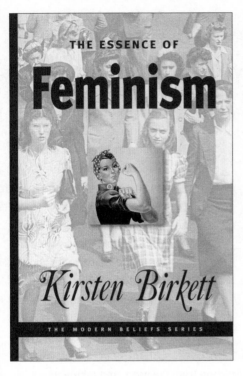

Feminism has permeated the modern world—it affects how we act, how we think, how we speak. It is one of the most powerful forces in Western society. How did it get to be that way? Are its claims true and are its arguments valid?

In this book, Kirsten Birkett has researched the origins of modern feminism, what it fought for and what it has achieved. She began writing the book considering herself a feminist. By the end, she was no longer one and this book explains why.

The Essence of Feminism is certain to challenge and educate its readers. It is required reading for anyone seeking to understand and respond to the most significant social movement of our generation.

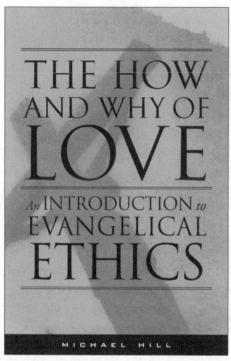